THE CONCEPT OF PUBLIC ORDER

The writing of this dissertation was conducted under the direction of the Reverend Romaeus W. O'Brien, O. Carm., M.A., J.C.D., as major professor, and was approved by the Reverend Frederick R. McManus, A.B., J.C.D. and the Reverend John J. McGrath, A.B., LL.B., J.C.D., as readers.

THE CATHOLIC UNIVERSITY OF AMERICA
CANON LAW STUDIES
No. 399

# The Concept of Public Order

A DISSERTATION

*Submitted to the Faculty of the School of Canon Law of The Catholic University of America in Partial Fulfillment of the Requirements for the Degree of Doctor of Canon Law*

BY

JOHN HENRY HACKETT, A.B., J.C.L.
*Priest of the Diocese of Fall River*

THE CATHOLIC UNIVERSITY OF AMERICA PRESS
WASHINGTON, D. C.
1959

NIHIL OBSTAT:

Romaeus G. O'Brien, O. Carm., M.A., J.C.D.
*Censor Deputatus*
Washingtonii, die 30 aprilis 1958

IMPRIMATUR:

✠ Iacobus L. Connolly, D.D., Dr. Sc. Hist.
*Episcopus Riverormensis*
Riverormi, die 9 iunii 1958


*Printed by Sullivan Bros., Printers, Lowell, Massachusetts, U.S.A.*

# FOREWORD

The appearance of the term *public order* in the Code of Canon Law[1] at once arouses interest and prompts a question. The question concerns the sense in which the term is used, for its meaning is not immediately evident. The special interest concerns the source of the term, for its use by canonists is comparatively recent. Very likely the term was borrowed from civil law. If this is so, it indicates one of the points of contact between the two legal systems.

The Code of Canon Law employs the term first[2] with reference to the traveller's subjection to local statutes. Canon 14 establishes the general principle favoring the traveller's freedom and the exceptional instances in which he is under the same obligation as the resident. In many civil systems provisions like this are to be found regulating the conduct of the alien. Questions concerning the alien's subjection to local statutes are commonly designated conflicts of law. Solution of these conflicts is one of the objects of Private International Law. Civil jurists have proposed various theories to govern the relationship between the alien and the laws of the country he visits, and the doctrine of public order is fundamental to many of these. It is not surprising to find the same term is used in resolving similar conflicts of canon law.

However, one must not readily assume that the doctrine of public order is the same in both canon and civil law. Problems arising from the relationship between the traveller and the local superior have proved vexing to canonists over the centuries. Those who, in the last sixty or more years, have introduced the term into their study of these problems must have regarded it as an appropriate designation for the careful distinctions that had been drawn to safeguard the rights of the traveller and the welfare of the community. Thus it would be a mistake to interpret public order in the light of civil jurisprudence, although this seems to be the source of the term.

[1] "Peregrini . . . non adstringuntur . . . legibus territorii in quo versantur, iis exceptis quae ordini publico consulunt . . . ."—can. 14, § 1, 2°.

[2] See also can. 141, § 1: " . [clerici ne] intestinis bellis et ordinis publici perturbationibus opem quoque modo ferant."

Rather, its meaning must be understood in the light of canonical doctrine as it developed over the course of many years. The key to a proper understanding of the term is to be found in the canonical principles concerning the relationship that exists between law and the person or the territory for which it is enacted.

While public order is a general notion having other applications in the field of law, it is frequently used in the solution of conflicts of law. A correct concept of public order is necessary for the traveller who wishes to understand the extent of his obligation with respect to local statutes. It is equally necessary for the superior who wishes to understand the extent to which he may lawfully act in legislating for those who ordinarily are not his subjects.

It is a pleasure to have this opportunity to express my sincere gratitude to His Excellency, the Most Reverend James L. Connolly, D.D., Dr.Sc.Hist., Bishop of Fall River, for the opportunity to undertake graduate studies and for his continued kindness; and to offer my thanks to the Faculty of the School of Canon Law, the Catholic University of America, for their generous and valuable assistance.

TABLE OF CONTENTS

# INTRODUCTION

The term *public order* first occurs in the Code of Canon Law with reference to the traveller's obligation to conform to local statutes.[3] The extent of this obligation is a question that ultimately concerns the very nature of law. There is a bond that exists between the law and the territory for which it is enacted as well as between the law and the person to whom it is directed. As long as the subject remains in the place where the law is established, no conflict arises. When the subject goes to another place which has a system of laws proper to itself, the jurist must decide whether the person is bound to obey his own superior or the ruler of the place he visits. Two bonds exist, and the jurist must decide which prevails: the one that exists between the person and the laws of his own superior, or the one that exists between the place at hand and the laws that have been enacted for its order and well-being. This is a question with which canonists have been concerned since the beginnings of the scientific study of church law.

The decretists and the decretalists wrote of the traveller with respect to the observance of local laws of fast, abstinence, and attendance at Mass. Their diverse opinions, based mostly upon inconclusive arguments from authority, afford little help in discerning a consistent theory of the extent of jurisdiction.[4]

Boniface VIII (1294-1303) gave the canonists fresh material for speculation. In the decretal *Ut animarum* he declared:

> Statuto episcopi, quo in omnes qui furtum commiserint, excommunicationis sententia promulgatur, subditi eius, furtum

[3] Can. 14, § 1, 2°

[4] The decretists and decretalists came to contrary conclusions regarding the traveller's subjection to local laws. For the most part they appealed to the authority of conflicting canons and decretals, especially *Quisquis,* (c. 1, D. XLI), *Quae contra* (c. 2, D. VIII), and *Illa* (c. 11, D. XII) in *Decretum Gratiani* and *A nobis* (c. 21, X, *de sententia excommunicationis,* V, 39), *De illis* (c. 1, X, *de raptoribus,* V, 17), *Postulasti* (c. 14, X, *de foro competenti,* II, 2), and *Licet* (e. 11, X, *de foro competenti,* II, 2) in the Decretals of Gregory IX.

extra ipsius dioecesim committentes, minime ligari noscuntur, quum extra territorium ius dicenti non pareatur impune.[5]

This decretal served as the basis for the principle canonists adopted that local statutes do not bind subjects who are outside the territory for which they have been enacted.

The Pontiff referred in his decretal to the dictum of the Roman jurist Paulus: *"Extra territorium ius dicenti impune non paretur. Idem est et si supra iurisdictionem suam velit ius dicere."*[6] The fragment is taken from his first book *Ad edictum*. It has reference to the limitations placed upon the jurisdiction of local magistrates. Properly speaking, this was contentious jurisdiction. It did not include the power to make law.

Paulus had in mind the case in which the magistrate was outside the territory over which he had charge.[7] Later the glossators extended the rule to include cases in which the subject or the possessions contested were to be found in a place beyond the magistrate's jurisdiction.[8]

Boniface VIII applied the dictum of Paulus with reference to the subject who is outside the territory for which a local law is enacted. He ruled that, whenever the subject acts contrary to the law in these circumstances, he does not incur the penalty it establishes.

Joannes Andreae (*c.* 1270-1348), in his gloss on the *Liber Sextus,* extended the decretal into the general rule that episcopal statutes do not bind the subject while he is outside the diocese.[9] Thereafter canonists commonly accepted the doctrine that local statutes are by nature territorial, for the legislator's jurisdiction is limited to the borders of his territory. Suarez and his followers held that all local

[5] C. 2, *de constitutionibus,* I, 2, in VI°.

[6] D. (2,1) 20.

[7] Cf. Wenger, *Institutes of the Roman Law of Civil Procedure* (rev. ed., translated by Otis Harrison Fisk, New York: Veritas, 1940), p. 39.

[8] "Sive dicas inter non suos subditos, sive inter suos subditos, de possessionibus quae sunt in alterius territorio, in quibus vult facere executionem . . sive etiam inter suos et de rebus intra territorium, ipse tamen est extra territorium quando iudicat, ut supra, de officio praefecti urbis. in fine [D. (1,12) 3], et hoc in contensiosa iurisdictione, in voluntaria secus . . "—Glossa ordinaria ad D. (2,1) 20, s. v. *non paretur.*

[9] ". . . quod statutum Episcopi extra suam dioecesim subditum non ligat." — Summarium ad c. 2, *de constitutionibus,* I, 2.

laws are fully territorial, even to the extent that they bind those who are not subject to a superior by reason of residence, but happen to be present, however briefly, in his place of jurisdiction. Sanchez and his followers taught that particular laws bind every subject while he is present in the territory, but they do not generally extend themselves to include the traveller.

Neither school of jurists found its principle to be perfectly satisfactory. Both had to admit that sometimes laws oblige the inhabitant even while he is absent. Suarez was faced with the problem of explaining how the ruler's jurisdiction over strangers is the same as that which he exercises over his subjects. Sanchez found it necessary to admit that in exceptional cases the traveller comes under local jurisdiction. They agreed that the ruler must protect the community, and they appealed to this as the reason for which he can exercise jurisdiction over the traveller.

The Code of Canon Law has adopted the teaching of Sanchez that the traveller is bound only by exception to observe local statutes. The reason for his subjection lies in the need to secure public order. The extraordinary grant of legislative jurisdiction is made so that the superior may protect the community from harm.

While the present law has adopted a relatively new term to designate this important responsibility, the idea is not new. It follows from the nature of law and society that the superior must guard the community entrusted to his care. The true notion of public order and the laws that tend to maintain it will be seen in light of the teachings of Suarez, Sanchez, and other canonists who have developed the theory upon which our present legal system is based.

# CHAPTER I

## THE TRAVELLER AND THE LOCAL STATUTE

In the sixteenth century moralists and canonists developed the doctrine of the traveller's obligation in respect to local statutes. Some regarded statutes to be territorial in character to the extent that they oblige everyone present. Thus Martin of Azpilcueta (Navarrus, 1493-1586),[10] Didacus Covarruvias y Leyva (1512-1587),[11] and Emmanuel Sa (1530-1596)[12] discussed this obligation in reference to attendance at Mass and observance of the fast. It remained for Suarez to develop a complete theory of the traveller's obligation to conform to all local statutes.

Others regarded statutes to be territorial, but in the restricted sense that they do not generally oblige the traveller. Thus Joannes de Medina (1490-1546),[13] Bartholomaeus de Medina (1528-1580),[14] and others taught that the ruler lacks jurisdiction over the traveller. Sanchez and others who followed his doctrine developed the theory to support this teaching. The present disposition of law is largely drawn from the teachings of Suarez, Sanchez, and later authors, and it is in the light of their doctrine that it must be understood.

### Article I. Doctrine of Francis Suarez

Francis Suarez (1548-1617), in addition to being a philosopher and theologian, was a distinguished jurist. Principally in his tract *De Legibus ac de Deo Legislatore* he presented his own teaching on the nature of law and a commentary on the doctrine of St. Thomas.

[10] *Enchridion sive Manuale Confessariorum et Poenitentium* (Wirceburgi, 1593), III, C. XIII, n. 5; et XXIII, n. 120.

[11] *Opera Omnia* (2 vols., Coloniae, 1579), II (*Variarum Resolutionum Libri Quatuor*), cap. 20, n. 8.

[12] *Aphorismi Confessariorum ex Variis Doctorum Sententiis* (ed. novissima, Lugduni, 1669), s.v. *festum*, n. 9; *ieiunium*, n. 1.

[13] *De Poenitentia, Restitutione, et Contractibus* (2 vols. in 1, Ingolstadii, 1581), I, tractatus IV (*Codex de ieiunio*), q. 10.

[14] *Expositio in I-IIae Angelici Doctoris D. Thomae Aquinatis* (Venetiis, 1590), q. 98, a. 6, *ad ultimum argumentum Cajetani*, p. 517.

According to Suarez, every perfect society enjoys the power to govern.[15] The law seeks to maintain order, peace, and tranquillity in the community, and in this way insure that the society will achieve the purpose for which it exists. The rule of law is vital to the community, and no subject is above it. Not every law obliges all, but the law reaches out to bind the individuals for whom it is intended by reason of their membership in the community.[16]

The bond which establishes this membership varies according to the nature of the society. Suarez compared the body politic with a natural body. Its members are joined in a moral rather than physical union. In civil society natural origin produces this relationship, while it is baptism that makes us members of the Church, and our relationship with a particular locality is determined by the acquisition or change of domicile. Members are received into other societies by a special act, such as religious profession. In these ways a person enters into a more or less permanent relationship with the society and becomes subject to its superior. He is bound to obey its laws inasmuch as these contribute to the welfare of all. His obligation flows from the superior's jurisdiction, for the right to command supposes a corresponding obligation to obey.[17] It is also possible for a person to enter a transient relationship with the community. This

[15] ". . . sicut communitas perfecta est rationi et naturali iuri consentanea, ita et potestas gubernandi illam, sine qua esset summa confusio in tali communitate." — *Opera Omnia* (26 vols., Parisiis, 1856-1866), V (*Tractatus de Legibus ac de Deo Legislatore*), III, c. I, n. 4 (hereafter cited as *De Legibus*).

[16] ". . . quia lex . . . per se primo fertur in communitatem, et inde descendit eius obligatio ad singulos."—*De Legibus*, III, c. XXXI, n. 6.

[17] "Respondetur . . . sicut in naturali corpore actualia membra constituuntur per unionem proportiatum tali corpori . . ita in corpore politico membra constitui per moralem coniunctionem, quae non est eiusdem rationis in omnibus communitatibus, sed cum proportione sumenda est: nam in civili republica, postquam semel constituta est, ordinarie constitui solent membra per naturalem originem . . . . In Ecclesia vero universali constituuntur membra per spiritualem originem, nempe Baptismum; in particulari vero per mutationem vel acquisitionem domicilii . . . . In aliis vero specialibus communitatibus solent constitui membra per specialem receptionem, seu acceptionem in collegam, et per aliquam promissionem, vel iuramentum, ut constat in universitatibus, collegiis, capitulis, religionibus, et similibus: haec autem intelligenda sunt de unione et subiectione quasi permanente; nam transeunter (ut sic dicam) possunt dari alii modi contrahendi subiectionem, ut inferius explicabitur." — *Ibid.*, n. 7.

is the status of the traveller, whose obligations with respect to the local superior Suarez later discussed in great detail.[18]

Suarez taught that a legislator whose jurisdiction is limited to a certain territory can make laws for that place and no other. Such laws look first to the place for which they have been created and seek to safeguard its peace and protect its customs. They affect the individual only secondarily and through the medium of the locality.[19]

A person's subjection to local laws, whether ecclesiastical or civil, depends upon his residence and the place in which he happens to be present. The inhabitant is bound to observe the laws of his own territory while he is there. When he leaves it, he is no longer bound, for the legislator has the power to make laws only in and for the territory over which he rules.[20]

The traveller must observe all the laws in force in the place he visits, for the law binds its subjects in and through the territory.[21] This is necessary for the peace and order of the community and the avoidance of scandal.[22]

[18] Cf. *infra*, pp. 4-7.

[19] "Statutum directe ac per se respicit territorium et pacem illius vel communes mores eius, ut in eo servandi sunt, et ideo non cadit in personas etiam subditas, nisi ut existentes intra territorium. Et ita in eodem capite [*Ut animarum*, Statuto, De Const. in 6 (c. 2, *de constitutionibus*, I, 2, in VI°)] additur ratio: Quia extra territorium ius dicenti non paretur impune. Nam cum iurisdictio, ut respicit territorium, intra illud limitetur, lex quae pro territorio fertur, non potest extra illud obligare quia excederet iurisdictionem."—*Opera Omnia*, XIII-XIV (*Opus de Virtute et Statu Religionis*), tractatus II, liber II, caput XIII, n. 2 (hereafter cited as *De Virtute Religionis*).

[20] "Nihilominus dicendum est legem non obligare extra terminum territorii illius superioris vel principis a quo fertur, et ideo incolas illius territorii, per se loquendo nihil peccare etiamsi contra illum agant, dum extra territorium existunt. Haec est communis sententia doctorum in c. 2, de Constit. in VI° [c. 2, *de constitutionibus*, I, 2, in VI°] et in dicto cap. *A nobis*, 1, de Sententia excommunicationis [c. 2, X, *de sententia excommunicationis*, V, 39]."—*De Legibus*, III, c. XXXII, n. 3.

[21] ". . . lex generatim fertur pro tali territorio, . ergo obligat omnes actu ibi degentes pro tempore quo ibi commorantur."—*De Legibus*, III, c. XXXIII, n. 3.

[22] "Nihilominus dicendum est legem territorii obligare advenas quamdiu ibi commorantur, in conscientia, et eo modo quo obligat incolas. Propria vero ratio est, quia lex generaliter fertur pro tali territorio, ut supponimus: ergo obligat

It is unreasonable to say that only one having a domicile in a particular place is bound to observe its laws. The same obligation arises from residence for a shorter time. Suarez rejected the teaching that the intention to reside for the greater part of a year is required to establish quasi-domicile. He adopted the opinion of Martin of Azpilcueta that an indefinite period is sufficient. While residence of four or five months would certainly suffice, common estimation is the essential norm of quasi-domicile. It is only necessary that the visitor have the intention to remain long enough that he might reasonably be called an inhabitant.[23] By this fact he acquires a quasi-domicile and becomes a subject of the local ruler.

Even the traveller who is merely passing through a locality is bound to observe its laws to the extent that time allows. That is to say, he is not obliged to delay his journey to fulfill a local law. Thus a person who is passing through a town where there exists a local precept to hear Mass need not delay his journey to comply with this statute. If he should remain there for a greater part of the morning, he would be under the same obligation as the inhabitants. The obligation is based upon public necessity. The peace and order of the community require that its laws be obeyed by the traveller

omnes actu ibi degentes pro tempore quo ibi commorantur. Probatur consequentia, primo, ex parte causae finalis, quia ad bonam gubernationem provinciae, loci, seu territorii, est moraliter necessarium ut leges pro illo latae hanc vim habeant; quia ad pacem et bonos mores loci necesse est ut advenae conformentur moribus populi, quamdiu ibi versantur, ut saepe in jure insinuatur, cap. *Illud,* distinct, 12 [c. 4, D. XII], cap. *Quae contra,* distinct. 8 [c. 2, D. VIII], cap. *In nova,* 16, quaest. 7 [c. 22, C. XVI, q. 7], et experientia id satis docet, quia, si aliter fiat, sequuntur dissidia et scandala. Cum ergo leges ferantur propter commune bonum, et pacem et bonos mores loci praecipue intendant, necesse est ut hanc vim habeant. Secundo, idem probatur ex parte causae efficientis, seu potestatis legislatoris, quia unusquisque gubernator reipublicae habet potestatem necessariam ad conservationem suae reipublicae, et ad eius bonos mores tuendos; ergo habet potestatem ad ferendas leges quas omnes ibi morantes servare tenentur. Hac enim ratione habet potestatem puniendi advenas ibi delinquentes: ergo eadem ratione habet potestatem obligandi per suam legem omnes ibi operantes, quatenus ad bonum suae reipublicae necessarium est."—*Loc. cit.*

[23] "Unde placet mihi quod Navarrus . . . dicit satis esse accedere cum animo habitandi ibi ad tempus incertum . . . adeo magnum ut arbitrio prudentis possit dici esse habitator."—*De Virtute Religionis,* tract. II, lib. II, c. XIV, n. 6.

who is visiting and the traveller who is merely passing through the territory.[24]

Suarez analyzed the basis for this obligation. The traveller who comes to a locality with the intention of remaining there for an indefinite period, one which gives rise to the common opinion that he is a resident, is subject to local laws by reason of quasi-domicile. The traveller who remains only for a few days acquires no quasi-domicile, yet he too is bound.[25] The reason lies in the needs of the community. Good government demands that all laws be observed in a uniform manner.[26] Therefore it is within the power of every ruler to oblige the traveller to conform to local laws.[27] For there is a danger that if the traveller does not obey local laws, the residents will be led to follow his example. Suarez declared that this danger of scandal is present in the case of every local law and custom. Public necessity demands uniform observance of the law in each instance. The extension of the bishop's jurisdiction to include travellers is demanded for the peace and good order of the community.[28]

He pointed out that this teaching finds confirmation in the practice

[24] *Ibid.*, n. 18.

[25] ". . . nec iurisdictio nec subiectio desit et in citato loco de censuris *(Opera Omnia*, XIII (*De Censuris*), disp. V, sect. 5 (hereafter cited as *De Censuris*)], singillatim ostendimus ad hanc obligationem sufficere imprimis quasi-domicilium, deinde satis esse brevem moram aliquorum dierum, et hanc extendendam esse cum proportione ad viatores qui ad breve tempus in hospitio commorantur . . . ."—*De Legibus*, III, c. XXXIII, n. 5.

[26] ". . quia ad bonam gubernationem provinciae, loci, vel territorii est moraliter necessarium ut leges pro illo latae hanc vim habeant; quia ad pacem et bonos mores loci necesse est ut advenae conformentur moribus populi quamdiu ibi versantur . . . ."—*De Legibus*, III, c. XXXIII, n. 3.

[27] ". . . quia unusquisque gubernator reipublicae habet potestatem necessariam ad conservationem suae reipublicae, et ad eius bonos mores tuendos; ergo habet potestatem ad ferendas leges quas omnes ibi morantes servare tenentur."—*Loc. cit.*

[28] "Dicis satis esse quod peregrini ex iure naturali teneantur ad scandalum vitandum. Sed contra, quia sicut ratio scandali obligat ex caritate, ita potest inde sumi ratio sufficiens ad praecipiendum vel prohibendum simpliciter . . . . Hoc ergo modo, ex scandalo quod moraliter timeri potest, si advenae non conformentur populo in observatione festi seu localis statuti, colligimus Episcopum loci, seu alium similem legislatorem habere ius et potestatem ad obligandum omnes qui actu degunt in tali loco, ad servandam legem et uniformitatem cum aliis, quia hoc est per se necessarium ad pacem et bonum regimen talis loci; ergo hac ratione illi advenae, quatenus ibi existunt, sunt subditi gubernatori loci, quatenus ad illum

of secular rulers. They often legislate for travellers in order to provide for the welfare of their land and people.[29]

Suarez considered it of sufficient importance to specify that the obligation of a traveller to observe a local law does not arise from the danger of scandal, but from the force of the law itself. For if scandal were its basis, the obligation would cease when the danger was no longer present, or when the traveller acted secretly.

On the contrary, the danger of scandal is the motive which causes the legislator to act, but the law binds of its own force. It continues to oblige the traveller even if the danger of scandal ceases.[30]

The legislator has the further power to make special laws for visitors. It is equally necessary for the welfare of the community that he should be able to legislate for travellers as a class.[31]

Finally, the legislator has the right to punish the traveller who violates his law. This is necessary if legislative power is to be effective.[32]

spectat paci talis loci consulere, et consequenter etiam statuere de moribus ad illam necessariis; ergo per se etiam et directe obligantur tali lege vel consuetudine."—*De Virtute Religionis,* trac. II, lib. II, cap. XIV, n. 11.

[29] "Confirmatur ex potestate principum laicorum . quia princeps laicus in multis casibus habet potestatem statuendi leges in terra sua, etiam in ordine ad peregrinos, quando respiciunt bonum et utilitatem suae terrae vel populi, in ordine ad externam iustitiam et pacem; ergo idem poterit Episcopus in ordine ad spirituale bonum."—*Ibid.*, n. 12.

[30] " . constat non recte aliquos dixisse teneri advenas ad has leges servandas solum propter vitandum scandalum. Hoc enim verum non est, alias, cessante scandalo, ac per se in occulto non obligarentur his legibus. Dicendum ergo est, licet interveniente actuali scandalo crescat accidentarie obligatio, non tamen esse scandalum proprium fundamentum obligationis, sed ad summum esse occasionem vel motivum, quod legislatorem movet ad ferendam legem cuius obligatio non cessat, etiamsi in particulari cesset motivum: sicut prohibentur arma in tali loco vel tempore ut vitentur rixae, et prohibentur feminae hoc vel illo modo ornari, ut non praebeant scandalum; et nihilominus, postquam leges positae sunt, obligatio non est tantum scandali, sed per se ratione talium legum."—*De Legibus,* III, c. XXXIII, n. 6.

[31] " . nam ad bonum civitatis vel reipublicae spectat ordinare quomodo peregrini se ibi gerere debeant, et statuere quae ad hunc finem necessaria fuerint, alioqui non fuisset sufficienter provisum reipublicae . . "—*Ibid.*, n. 7.

[32] "Et ratio est manifesta, quia idem titulus subiectionis seu potestatis intervenit quoad vim coactivam, qui demonstratus est de vi directiva: imo directiva non esset efficax nisi haberet adiunctam coactivam."—*Ibid.*, n. 9.

After explaining the extent of the legislator's jurisdiction over the traveller, Suarez tried to discover its foundation. It clearly does not arise from domicile or quasi-domicile, yet Suarez was convinced that such jurisdiction is essential and must have a juridic source. He regarded the practice of subjecting the traveller to local statutes as being universally recognized. It is not properly founded in *ius gentium,* yet it seems to be acknowledged by the faithful, the bishops, and the Roman Pontiffs. He judged it to be true episcopal jurisdiction arising *"quasi ex iure gentium."*[33]

## Article II. Doctrine of Thomas Sanchez and Followers

### A. Thomas Sanchez

Thomas Sanchez (1551-1610) was a contemporary of Suarez. He taught at Cordova. In 1602, thus ten years before the appearance of Suarez' *De Legibus,* he published a lengthy treatise on matrimony. In the course of this work he discussed the obligation of the traveller to observe local laws. The question was of special importance in view of the law of the Council of Trent concerning the canonical form of marriage. Where the law was promulgated, it affected the validity of the marriage contract. Where it had not been promulgated, its provisions were not in force. Sanchez discussed the principles bearing upon the traveller's obligations in order to clarify the extent to which he was bound to observe the Tridentine legislation concerning the form of marriage.

Sanchez taught that the traveller is bound to observe local laws that are also in force in his domicile. Since the law exists in both places, he could see no cause that would excuse the traveller.

[33] "Unde videtur dicendum, illam consuetudinem ut advenae commorantes per aliquos dies in uno loco se conforment moribus loci in his quae ad communem vitam spectant, esse quasi ex iure gentium, et inde habere vim suam; tamen quia obligatio . . . non est immediate ex iure gentium, sed ex statuto talis episcopatus, necesse est dicere, quasi communi iure gentium, et ex consensu omnium fidelium, et praecipue pastorum et Pontificum, introductum in ecclesiam esse, ut Episcopi possunt, suis statutis obligare, non solum incolas, sed omnes ad tempus aliquod habitantes in suis dioecesibus, vel locis sibi subiectis; ergo supposita illa consuetudine universali, et quasi iure gentium obligatio est ex vi iurisdictionis episcopalis."—*De Virtute Religionis,* tract. II, lib. II, cap. XIV, n. 10.

He further acknowledged that the traveller is obliged to conform to local practice when this is necessary to prevent scandal.[34]

However, scandal does not invariably follow from the violation of a law. The stranger can explain to bystanders that he is not bound by their laws, or he can act in secret.[35] In either case, it is not likely that his conduct will mislead others. Consequently, his obligation to obey local laws in these circumstances is questionable.

The more probable opinion, according to Sanchez, is that generally the traveller is not bound to observe local laws and customs when they do not oblige also in his own domicile, and there is no danger that his conduct will give scandal.[36] It is interesting to observe how he reasoned to this conclusion. For, like Suarez, he held that the binding force of law is closely associated with the territory for which it is enacted. The law binds those for whom it is intended who are actually present. The traveller is present for so short a time that Sanchez regarded him as morally absent from the place. Since he is not morally present in the territory, he is not obliged to observe its laws, as a general rule.[37]

The person who remains in a territory for a sufficient length of time is under the same obligations as the inhabitant. Sanchez taught that one who intends to reside in a place for the greater part of a year is bound by its laws. He thereby acquires a quasi-domicile.

[34] "Similiter certum est [peregrinos] licet divertant per modum transitus, si consuetudines et leges sui oppidi ibi etiam obligant, teneri ad eas, quia nulla est ratio excusans      Deinde certum est, ratione scandali, si forte orietur legibus loci transitus non servatis, teneri transeuntes eas servare."—*Disputationum de Sancto Matrimonii Sacramento Libri Decem* (3 vols., Venetiis, 1607), III, disp. XVIII, n. 3 (hereafter cited as *De Matrimonio*).

[35] "Difficultas autem est, quando peregrini divertunt per modum transitus, aut hospitii ad huiusmodi loca, an cessante scandalo (quod facile vitari potest admonitis adstantibus se non teneri ad eas leges, vel occulte transgrediendo) teneantur servare leges vel consuetudines loci, in quo per modum transitus reperiuntur, quando eae in suo domicilio non obligant?"—*Ibid.*, n. 4.

[36] "Sententia probabilior ait peregrinos et forenses non adstringi legibus aut consuetudinibus loci per quem transeunt, vel in quo per modum hospitii reperiuntur, cessante scandalo, et quando eae non obligant in suo domicilio."—*Ibid.*, n. 6.

[37] ". . quia qui transit aut brevi tempore divertit ad locum, non dicitur moraliter in eo esse      . Si ergo transeuntes non dicuntur moraliter esse in eo loco, minime aequum est ut ipsius loci leges observare astringuntur: cum solos in eo existentes obligant."—*Loc. cit.*

His obligation begins the moment he takes up residence. It is not necessary that the time should have elapsed, but only that he intends to reside there for the required period.[38]

Thus the general rule may be laid down that the traveller is exempt from local laws and customs, for he does not fall under the jurisdiction of the legislator by reason of domicile or quasi-domicile. Yet the rule admits of exceptions.

The first exception has reference to contractual formalities. If the traveller wishes to make a valid contract, he must observe the requirements of the locality.[39]

The second exception concerns actions that will work a harm to the community. The traveller is not free to transgress a law if it results in an injury to the locality. For example, he may not take from a town certain objects prohibited by law. He may not remain in a town longer than the law allows.[40] The reason the traveller is bound to observe such laws and customs is to be found in the public good. The welfare of the community requires that travellers observe some of its laws. Laws which do not affect the public good do not impose an obligation upon the traveller, apart from the natural obligation that would arise if the danger of scandal were present.[41]

The third exception to the general rule excusing travellers from local laws refers to those who have no place of residence. They are obliged to observe all local laws. Since they have no domicile,

[38] "Unde credo sufficere ut aliquis teneatur legibus et consuetudinibus alicuius oppidi, ut maiori anni parte ibi sit habitaturus: hoc enim sufficiens est ad constituendum domicilium, non simpliciter, sed quasi-domicilium ad sacramenta necessaria . . . . Id autem observandum est, eo animo habitandi per majorem anni partem, accedentem, teneri a prima die accessus, servare consuetudines et leges illius oppidi . . ."—*Ibid.*, n. 9.

[39] *Ibid.*, n. 10.

[40] "Secunda exceptio est, nisi legum transgressio cederet in damnum illius oppidi, tunc enim peregrinus illis tenetur: ut si sint aliquae leges prohibentes aliquid extrahi ex illo oppido, vel ne viatores ibi commorentur, nisi tot diebus, in bonum illius oppidi."—*Ibid.*, n. 14.

[41] ". . . [quia bonum civitatis publicum postulat ut uniuscuiuscumque oppidi consuetudines observentur, tam ab incolis quam a peregrinis, dum in eo sunt] quando leges disponunt circa bonum et utilitatem ipsius reipublicae, quare tunc peregrini tenentur eas servare . . Circa alias autem leges nil interest boni illius reipublicae, ut peregrini eas observent, cessante scandalo."—*Ibid.*, n. 16.

Sanchez taught that they acquire one wherever they are. It is effective in all respects, just as if acquired by permanent residence. In this way Sanchez avoided what he regarded as the incongruous situation in which they would generally be excused from particular laws in that they have no domicile of their own and are obliged only in an exceptional way to observe the laws of the place in which they are present.[42]

### B. Paul Laymann

Paul Laymann (1574-1635) was a professor at Ingolstadt.[43] In his posthumous work *Theologia Moralis* he examined the obligations of the traveller in respect to local laws.

Following Suarez and Navarrus, he taught that quasi-domicile may be acquired by residence of an indeterminate time. One who intends to remain in a place long enough to be regarded as an inhabitant acquire a quasi-domicile and consequent subjection to local legislation.[44]

Nevertheless, he adhered to the teaching of Sanchez that as a general rule the traveller who remains only for a short time is excused from the obligation of observing local laws. The reason lies in lack of jurisdiction on the part of the legislator.[45]

Suarez had maintained that the law reaches its subjects through the medium of the territory. It obliges all who are in the territory,

[42] "Tertia exceptio est, ut non intelligatur de vagis, qui nullibi certam sedem habent: hi enim tenentur ad leges et consuetudines loci in quo etiam obiter reperiuntur. Probatur, quia cum nullum peculiariter domicilium habeant, illum quoad omnia acquirunt ubicumque reperiuntur. Item quia alias viderentur exempti ab omnibus statutis et consuetudinibus ..."—*Ibid.*, n. 15.

[43] Van Hove, *Commentarium Lovaniense in Codicem Iuris Canonici* (1 vol. in 5 toms., Mechliniae—Romae: H. Dessain, 1928-1939), Tom. I, *Prolegomena* (editio altera, 1945), 537, 567.

[44] *Theologia Moralis* (6. ed., 2 vols., Bambergae, 1669), I, tract. IV, cap. XII, n. 1.

[45] "Advenae et peregrini, dum in aliena terra non inhabitandi, sed tantum hospitandi causa adsunt, non obligantur legibus et consuetudinibus eius loci propriis et specialibus ... Ratio est quia ad obligandum aliquem legibus, requiritur iurisdictio: sed peregrini ob brevem hospitii moram non subiiciuntur iurisdictioni, seu non acquirunt forum sicuti constat ex 1. *haeres absens* supra citata [D. (5,1) 19]."—*Ibid.*, n. 4.

residents and travellers alike.[46] Laymann rejected this idea. He explained that the territorial aspect of law is more properly understood in the sense that the law touches only those in the locality who are under the jurisdiction of the legislator. As a rule the traveller is excluded.[47]

He agreed with Sanchez that there are exceptional cases in which the traveller becomes subject to local jurisdiction. He is bound by those laws which provide in a special way for the good and welfare of the community. He must obey those local laws that assure peaceful association with the inhabitants. He is bound to observe local contractual formalities. Apart from this, however, the traveller is free of the obligation which local laws impose, for there is no reason to regard him as subject to the jurisdiction of the local superior. He has no domicile or quasi-domicile. His subjection can not arise by reason of crime, for he can commit no crime until he is first bound by law.[48]

On the same basis of lack of jurisdiction Laymann took issue with Soto (*c.* 1494-1560),[49] Suarez,[50] and Sanchez,[51] regarding the status of persons having neither domicile nor quasi-domicile. He

[46] Cf. *supra,* p. 3, n. 21.

[47] ". . . leges locales esse, id est locum afficere, indeque transire in habitantes qui iurisdictioni eius loci subiecti sunt; non autem in alienigenas et peregrinos."—*Ibid.*, n. 5, ad tertiam.

[48] "A tertia nostra assertione [i.e. 'leges locales esse indeque transire in habitantes non autem in alienigenas et peregrinos'—cf. *supra,* n. 47] excipiendas esse eas leges quae specialiter servuntur ob bonum et utilitatem talis reipublicae vel ob pacificam communicationem cum incolis. Eiusmodi enim leges peregrini quoque servare tenentur, sicuti ex Legistarum doctrina bene admonet Sanchez, citata disputatione 18, numero 14 [*De Matrimonio,* III, Disp. XVIII, n. 14—cf. *supra,* p. 9, n. 40]. Quo etiam pertinent leges contractuum, de quibus obiectio facta est. Porro allegatum cap. ult. [c. 20, X, *de foro competenti,* I, 2] prorsus confirmat nostram sententiam: dicitur enim ibi, quemvis sortiri forum vel ratione domicilii, vel ratione delicti, vel ratione contractus. Unde a contrario sensu inferre licet, si peregrinus neque domicilium habitationemve fixit, neque in loco deliquit, neque ibi contraxit, non sortiri forum, adeoque legibus et iurisdictioni subiectum non esse."—*Ibid.*, n. 5, ad quintum.

[49] *Commentarium in Quartum Sententiarum* (2 vols., Venetiis, 1569), II, ad lib. IV, dist. XVIII, q. 4, a. 2, *Est hic tamen.*

[50] *De Virtute Religionis,* tract. II, lib. II, cap. XIV n. 18.

[51] *Opus Morale in Praecepta Decalogi* (editio recens, 2 vols., Lugduni, 1661-1669) I, cap. 12, n. 23.

adopted the opinion mentioned as probable by Lessius (1554-1623)[52] that such a one is excused from the obligation of observing local laws on the ground that the legislator has no jurisdiction over him. His status is the same as that of the traveller who has a domicile in another place.[53]

### C. Lucius Ferraris

Lucius Ferraris (d. *c.* 1763) regarded as the common teaching of canonists the doctrine of Joannes Andreae[54] that the local ruler's jurisdiction is limited to the territory over which he rules. This had become the traditional interpretation of the decretal *Ut animarum.*[55] He further taught that the legislator's jurisdiction is limited to those within the locality who are actually his subjects. It does not generally extend to the travellers who are present.[56]

By way of exception, travellers are subject to local laws concerning the formation of contracts.[57] They are also subject to particular laws established to provide in a special way for the common good of the locality. Such laws would be the provisions of secular legislation that

[52] *De Iustitia et Iure Ceterisque Virtutibus Cardinalibus Libri Quatuor* (3. ed., Antverpiae, 1612), IV, cap. 2, dub. 7, n. 49.

[53] ". . . eamdem esse rationem vagorum, quae peregrinorum: ut non obligentur legibus propriis locorum in quibus hospitantur vel transeunt: quia generalis doctrina est ex capite ultimo. de foro competenti [c. 20, X, *de foro competenti*, I, 2] neminem sortiri forum nisi vel ratione domicilii, sive habitationis, vel ratione delicti, vel ratione contractus; adde tu vel ratione rei sive possessionis sitae in territorio, vel denique interdum ratione originis sive patriae . . . . Vagi autem nullo horum modorum subiecti sunt, ut ponimus. Ergo non sortitur forum."—*Ibid.*, n. 7.

[54] Cf. *supra*, p. x, n. 9.

[55] C. 2, *de constitutionibus*, I, 2, in VI°

[56] Ad leges et statuta inferiorum praelatorum ecclesiasticorum, aliorumque superiorum obligantur solum subditi proprii territorii. Communis. Ad obligationem enim legis necessaria est iurisdictio quam non habet legislator in non suos subditos; arg. 1. ult. de iurisdictione omnium iudicum [D. (2,1) 20] . . et concordat cap. ut animarum 2 de constitutionibus [c. 2, *de constitutionibus*, I, 2, in VI°]. Imo neque ad tales leges tenentur subditi, quando actu existunt extra territorium legislatoris . . . ."—*Prompta Bibliotheca, Canonica, Iuridica, Moralis, Theologica, necnon Ascetica, Polemica, Rubristica, Historica* (9 vols., Romae, 1885-1899), V, verbo *Lex*, art. III, nn. 11, 12 (hereafter cited as *Prompta Bibliotheca*).

[57] *Ibid.*, n. 12.

certain merchandise is not to be exported, restrictions on the expenditure of money, laws prohibiting the carrying of arms. Even travellers, when they violate such laws, are subject to punishment.[58]

### D. Francis Schmalzgrueber

Francis Schmalzgrueber (1663-1735) compared the two schools of canonical thought on the traveller's obligation in respect to local laws and customs. It was certain and accepted by all that the traveller must obey local laws if he establishes a domicile or quasi-domicile in the place where he stays.[59] All agreed that he is bound by the laws of the universal church that are in effect in the place he visits even if they have no force in his place of residence.[60] All agreed that the traveller must obey particular laws that are established for the welfare of the community by reason of public necessity. He repeated the customary examples from the civil law: the prohibition against carrying certain types of arms, the law forbidding the export of certain merchandise, regulations as to the length of time a traveller may extend his visit. The ruler's jurisdiction is extended in these cases because the welfare of the people demands it. He could not properly protect them unless these laws were observed by all.[61]

Suarez and others maintained further that the public welfare demands uniform observance of every local law, for peace, tranquillity, and good example are no less important to the community than are the regulation of commerce and arms.[62]

[58] "Peregrini et advenae tenentur ad leges locorum ubi reperiuntur, quando tales leges latae sunt specialiter ob bonum commune illorum locorum ubi sunt, v. gr. leges quae prohibent ne certae merces ex oppido evehantur, ne certae pecuniae expendantur, ne certa genera armorum deferantur, et huiusmodi; aliter si ipsas leges scienter transgrederentur, possunt puniri, ac alii inquilini, cum tunc ratione delicti fiant subditi, et sortiantur forum loci ubi delinquunt."—*Ibid.*, n. 45.

[59] *Ius Canonicum Universum,* (6 vols. in 8, Romae, 1843), Tomus Primus, Pars Prima, pars I, titulus II, n. 42.

[60] *Loc. cit.*

[61] "Certum est sic transeuntem obligari legibus etiam particularibus loci, si illae specialiter latae sint in bonum illius loci ob necessitatem reipublicae uti sunt quae prohibent ne certae merces ex oppido extrahantur, ne peregrini ultra tot dies commorentur, ne certum genus armorum feratur, etc., quia aliter populus defendi non potest, nisi omnes qui ibi existunt, leges istas observent."—*Loc. cit.*

[62] Cf. *supra*, p. 5, n. 28.

Schmalzgrueber pointed out that not every violation of a law disturbs the peace and tranquillity of a community. When such a disturbance is to be expected, everyone will be bound to prevent it by reason of a higher obligation. For the natural law obliges everyone to avoid giving scandal or inflicting harm upon others.[63] This provision of natural law suffices to make it reasonably sure the community will not be harmed by the conduct of visitors. It is only by exception that the ruler will have occasion to intervene by reason of public necessity. Therefore it is more probable that as a general rule travellers are not obliged to observe local laws. They are exempt because they are not members of the community nor subject to the jurisdiction of its superior.[64]

## E. St. Alphonsus Liguori

At the beginning of the eighteenth century both of these canonical doctrines were regarded as well-founded and tenable. Anacletus Reiffenstuel (1642-1703) acknowledged the probability of the opinion of Sanchez and Laymann, yet he held the opinion of Suarez to be more common and more probable.[65] He defended the opinion of Suarez that particular law binds its subjects in and through the territory for which it is enacted. Thus it touches the traveller equally with the inhabitant.[66] This extension of the legislator's jurisdiction

[63] ". . . nam quacumque non observatione legum territorialium turbatur pax et tranquillitas reipublicae vel si turbatur, obligatio erit eas servandi, non vi authoritatis, quam in talem peregrinum legislator ille non habet; sed vi legis naturalis, quae prohibet scandala et nocumenta."—*Ibid.*, n. 42, ad quintum.

[64] "Dicendum tamen probabilius huiusmodi peregrinos per se loquendo legibus particularibus loci non obligari: et hinc si in tali loco servetur ieiunium, secluso scandalo, peregrinus potest ibi vesci carnibus, et si ibi celebretur festum, potest missam omittere . Ratio est, quia lex per se non obligat, nisi subditos, et membra communitatis, cui fertur; atqui praedicti peregrini moraliter non censentur subditi, vel membra communitatis, per cuius territorium dumtaxat transeunt, cum brevis mora habeatur pro nulla . . ."—*Op. cit.*, Tomus Primus, Pars Prima, pars I, titulus II, n. 42.

[65] *Theologia Moralis* (iam dudum edita, 2 vols., Bassani, 1773-1780), I, tractatus II, disputatio III, n. 25.

[66] ". . . quia leges immediate censentur afficere locum seu territorium legislatoris, atque hinc in subditos ibidem existentes transire . . ergo hoc ipso quod peregrinus reperiatur in tali territorio, tenetur legibus particularibus illius loci, ac censeatur subditus domini illius territorii . . . ."—*Ibid.*, n. 26.

to include travellers is necessary for the tranquillity of the community.[67]

On the other hand, St. Alphonsus Liguori (1696-1787) regarded the opinion of Sanchez as more probable.[68] He agreed that the traveller is not subject to the particular legislator as a general rule. He is bound to observe local contractual formalities. He must also observe certain other laws, especially those which cannot be violated without harm to the community.[69]

### Article III. Evaluation

Suarez and Sanchez represent opposite schools of thought regarding the traveller's obligation to observe local laws. Suarez taught that the traveller is always bound to obey them, for he is under the same obligation as the inhabitant.[70] Sanchez taught that as a general rule he is not bound to obey such laws, for his subjection arises only in exceptional cases.[71] Apart from this, they agreed that the reason the superior has extended jurisdiction over the traveller is to be found in the need to protect the peace and tranquillity of the community.

The maintenance of peace is one of the foundations of law.[72] St. Augustine explained that peace is the tranquillity of order.[73] Peace and good order are the effects to which every law is in some way directed. However, there are certain acts that threaten the peace in a

[67] " . . quia hoc exigit quies reipublicae, quae alias ex diversis hominum moribus perturbaretur .''—*Ibid.*, n. 22.

[68] *Theologia Moralis* (14. ed., 4 vols., Bassani, 1836), I, tractatus II, caput II, dub. II, n. 156.

[69] " quia tenentur quibusdam legibus, maxime quarum violatio cederet in damnum et iniuriam illius loci, in quo morantur, ut etiam iis quae sunt de contractibus celebrandis.—*Ibid.*, dub. III.

[70] Cf. *supra*, pp. 1-7.

[71] Cf. *supra*, pp. 7-10.

[72] "Legis enim humanae finis est temporalis tranquillitas civitatis, ad quem finem pervenit lex cohibendo exteriores actus, quantum ad illa mala quae possunt perturbare pacificum statum civitatis."—S. Thomas de Aquino, *Summa Theologiae*, (Pars Prima et Prima Secundae, cura et studio Sac. Petri Caramello, Taurini—Romae: Marietti, 1950), I-IIae, q. 98, a. 1, c.

[73] *De Civitate Dei*, Liber XIX, Caput XIII, n. 1—Migne, *Patrologiae Cursus Completus*, Series Latina (221 vols., Parisiis, 1884-1885), 41, 640 (hereafter cited as *MPL*).

special way, for they affect the society itself and not merely certain of its members. Suarez felt that, in addition to the effect it has upon the individuals concerned, every violation of law presents a danger to the community.[74] Sanchez was of the opinion that this was true only in exceptional cases.[75]

In either instance we must understand that when they referred, in this context, to the violation of a law as disruptive of the peace or inflicting harm upon the city, they did not mean the disorder that is implied in the very fact that a law is broken. They pointed rather to the social effect of the violation, to its influence upon the entire community.

The ruler's obligation to protect and defend the society that is entrusted to his care seems to be a principle recognized in every system of law. When this requires that he exercise jurisdiction over one ordinarily regarded not to be his subject, right reason demands that he should have the special authority to do so. Otherwise his office would impose an impossible burden upon him. Just as the ruler must act to prevent a hostile nation from harming his country, so he must forestall harm that would result from the misconduct of private individuals. Evident necessity gives him the power to do so by conferring upon him the jurisdiction to make a law that will bind the traveller as effectively as it binds the inhabitant. Consequently, it is important to know by what acts a private individual threatens harm to the community.

Suarez mentioned the danger that scandal presents to good conduct in the community. The virtue of charity requires that each

[74] "Hoc ergo modo, ex scandalo quod moraliter timeri potest, si advenae non conformentur populo in observatione festi seu localis statuti, colligimus Episcopum loci, seu alium similem legislatorem habere ius et potestatem ad obligandum omnes qui actu degunt in tali loco, ad servandam legem et uniformitatem cum aliis, quia hoc est per se necessarium ad pacem et bonum regimen talis loci . "—*De virtute Religionis*, tract. II, lib. II, cap. XIV, n. 11. Cf. *supra*, p. 5, n. 28.

[75] "Sententia probabilior ait peregrinos et forenses non adstringi legibus aut consuetudinibus loci per quem transeunt, vel in quo per modum hospitii repe-riuntur, cessante scandalo, et quando eae non obligant in suo domicilio."—*De Matrimonio*, III, disp. XVIII, n. 6. Cf. *supra*, p. 8, n. 36.

one should refrain from any act that gives scandal to another person. Charity, just as any other virtue, can be made the object of a command. Thus Suarez noted that the prior obligation of divine law does not rule out the superior's right to impose by human law a juridic obligation to refrain from acts that give scandal. The danger of spiritual ruin is a sufficient motive to enact such a law.[76] However, the law binds its own force. The element of scandal is only the motive for the law, not the source of the obligation to obey. Otherwise, the obligation would cease when the danger was removed.[77]

Suarez, of course, was of the opinion that the danger of scandal is present in the violation of every law. Peace and good order in the community require strict uniformity of conduct, lest one person, even a stranger, should lead others astray because he does not follow the laws and customs of the place.[78] Suarez maintained that this ever-present threat of scandal and discord gives the superior jurisdiction over everyone, traveller and subject alike.

Sanchez, on the contrary, taught that not every violation of law presents the threat of scandal. For the traveller who acts secretly, or who explains to the inhabitants that he is not bound by their law, causes no astonishment when he fails to conform to their customs. Since the danger of scandal is removed, the law of charity does not apply; and in the absence of any threat to the community, there is

[76] "Dicis satis esse quod peregrini ex iure naturali teneantur ad scandalum vitandum. Sed contra, quia sicut ratio scandali obligat ex caritate, ita potest inde sumi ratio sufficiens ad praecipiendum vel prohibendum simpliciter . . . ."—*De Virtute Religionis*, tract. II, lib. II, cap. XIV, n. 11. Cf. *supra*, p. 5, n. 28.

[77] "Non solum propter vitandum scandalum [tenentur advenae legibus loci] . . . Alias, cessante scandalo, ac per se in occulto non obligarentur his legibus. Dicendum ergo est, licet interveniente actuali scandalo crescat accidentarie obligatio, non tamen esse scandalum proprium fundamentum obligationis, sed ad summum esse occasionem vel motivum quod legislatorem movet ad ferendam legem cuius obligatio non cessat, etiamsi in particulari cesset motivum . . . ."—*Suarez, De Legibus*, III, c. XXXIII, n. 6. Cf. *supra*, p. 6, n. 30.

[78] ". . . quia ad bonam gubernationem provinciae, loci, vel territorii est moraliter necessarium ut leges pro illo latae hanc vim habeant; quia ad pacem et bonos mores loci necesse est ut advenae conformentur moribus populi quamdiu ibi versantur . . . ."—*Ibid*, n. 3. Cf. *supra*, p. 5, n. 26.

no basis for imposing a juridic obligation on the traveller. He is not a subject.[79]

We are not primarily interested to know whether the judgment of one or the other author, or perhaps both, represents an accurate evaluation of conditions in his own time and circumstances. What we must note is this. It is possible to conceive of a law that has for its direct purpose the removal of a source of public scandal, and a law that simply directs the subject in the exercise of one or another virtuous act. The former law seeks to remove a common spiritual danger; it is immediately concerned with the welfare of the community. The latter law has no more than a remote effect upon the community. One may assume that its violation will not cause widespread scandal; but if, by reason of special circumstances, the danger should arise, the traveller would be obliged to avoid it. This is the scandal to which Sanchez referred, a danger arising in an individual case, depending upon special circumstances, quite apart from the nature of the law broken. He did not have in mind the law that has for its direct purpose the removal of a danger threatening the entire society. When this is borne in mind it becomes clear that the words of one author complement rather than contradict the other.

It remained for Suarez to discuss the law that prohibits words or deeds directly tending to lead others into sin. Such conduct is a source of scandal and a peril to the whole community. Everyone is obliged by the law of charity to avoid giving this scandal, and the legislator adds to it a juridic obligation by enacting his prohibition. A law like this would extend its jurisdiction to the traveller and bind him equally with the inhabitant, for it seeks to destroy a source of scandal that is a threat to the community as well as to the individual.[80]

In addition to such spiritual danger a community can be injured in material ways, and the ruler has the same obligation and authority

[79] "Sententia probabilior ait peregrinos et forenses non adstringi legibus aut consuetudinibus loci per quem transeunt, vel in quo per modum hospitii reperiuntur, cessante scandalo ."—*De Matrimonio,* III, disp. XVIII, n. 6. Cf. *supra,* p. 8, n. 36.

[80] Cf. *supra,* p. 6, n. 30.

to provide protection. Statutes that prohibit the removal of certain objects from a town,[81] the export of merchandise or expenditure of money in a way that would imperil the community, the bearing of arms,[82] laws that limit the stay of an alien for the commonweal,[83] all have as their object the protection of society itself.[84] They seek to maintain the established order so that society will continue to be useful, that is to say, so that it will continue to serve the interests of the people. These laws are concerned directly with the welfare of the community itself, with the public good as distinguished from that of its members.[85]

[81] ". . . ut si sint aliquae leges prohibentes aliquid extrahi ex illo oppido . . "—Sanchez, *De Matrimonio,* III, disp. XVIII, n. 14. Cf. *supra,* p. 9, n. 40.

[82] " . . leges quae prohibent ne certae merces ex oppido evehantur, ne certae pecuniae expendantur, ne certa genera armorum deferantur, et huiusmodi . ."—Ferraris, *Prompta Bibliotheca,* V, verbo *Lex,* art. III, *n.* 45.—Cf. *supra,* p. 13; n. 58. ". . . sicut prohibentur arma in tali loco vel tempore ut vitentur rixae "—Suarez, *De Legibus,* III, c. XXXIII, n. 6.—Cf. *supra,* p. 6, n. 30.

[83] " ne viatores ibi commorentur, nisi tot diebus, in bonum illius oppidi "—Sanchez, *loc. cit.* Cf. *supra,* p. 9, n. 40.

[84] " . nisi legum transgressio cederet in damnum illius oppidi, tunc enim peregrinus illis tenetur."—Sanchez, *ibid.,* n. 14. Cf. *supra,* p. 9, n. 40. " . . quia tenentur quibusdam legibus, maxime quarum violatio cederet in damnum et iniuriam illius loci."—S. Alphonsus Liguori, *Theologia Moralis,* I, tract. II, cap. II, dub. III. Cf. *supra,* p. 15, n. 69.

[85] " [quia bonum civitatis publicum postulat ut uniuscuiuscumque oppidi consuetudines observentur, tam ab incolis quam a peregrinis, dum in eo sunt] quando leges disponunt circa bonum et utilitatem ipsius reipublicae . . Circa alias autem leges nihil interest boni illius reipublicae . . . "—Sanchez, *ibid.,* n. 16. Cf. *supra,* p. 9, n. 41. ". . . excipiendas esse eas leges quae specialiter servantur ob bonum et utilitatem talis reipublicae vel ob pacificam communicationem cum incolis."—Laymann, *Theologia Moralis,* I, tract. IV, cap. XII, n. 5, ad quintum. Cf. *supra,* p. 11, n. 48. ". . quando tales leges latae sunt specialiter ob bonum commune illorum locorum ubi sunt . "—Ferraris, *loc. cit.* Cf. *supra,* p. 13, n. 58. " . si illae specialiter latae sint in bonum illius loci ob necessitatem reipublicae . quia aliter populus defendi non potest nisi omnes qui ibi existunt leges istas observent."—Schmalzgrueber. *Ius Canonicum Universum,* Tomus Primus, Pars Prima, pars I, titulus II, n. 42. Cf. *supra,* p. 13, n. 61. " . . quia hoc exigit quies reipublicae, quae alias ex diversis hominum moribus perturbaretur "—Reiffenstuel, *Theologia Moralis,* I, tract. II, disp. III, q. III, n. 22. Cf. *supra,* p. 15, n. 67.

Sanchez mentioned as a distinct point that the traveller is bound to observe the contractual formalities required in the community.[86] This is a well-established provision of canon and civil law.[87] Laymann[88] and St. Alphonsus[89] seem to have regarded this as an obligation based upon public necessity. Although they mention specifically the traveller's subjection to local contractual formalities, they suggest that the peace and good order of the community would be upset if business relationships were not based upon uniform laws of contract.[90]

Clearly the examples given of laws that extend to the traveller and make him a subject are meant to serve only as illustrations. They demonstrate that society can suffer both spiritual and material harm. Inasmuch as this social disorder affects the entire community, it is an altogether exceptional peril and calls for exceptional measures of prevention. For this reason the superior can exercise jurisdiction over the traveller in order to see that he visits no harm upon the community.

Public necessity becomes an exceptional source of jurisdiction: exceptional because it goes beyond the limits of domicile and quasi-domicile to touch the stranger; and exceptional also, according to Sanchez and others, in that it confers this jurisdiction only in special circumstances to prevent harm from befalling the society itself.

[86] *Ibid.*, n. 10. See also Laymann, *Theologia Moralis,* I, tract. IV, cap. XII, n. 5; Ferraris, *Prompta Bibliotheca,* V, verbo *Lex,* art. III, n. 12.

[87] Cf. *infra,* pp. 55-58.

[88] ". . . excipiendas esse eas leges quae specialiter servuntur ob bonum et utilitatem talis reipublicae vel ob pacificam communicationem cum incolis . Quo etiam pertinent leges contractuum . . . "—*Loc. cit.* Cf. *supra,* p. 11, n. 48.

[89] ". . . quia tenentur quibusdam legibus, maxime quarum violatio cederet in damnum et iniuriam illius loci, in quo morantur, ut etiam iis quae sunt de contractibus celebrandis."—*Loc. cit.* Cf. *supra,* p. 15, n. 69.

[90] For an evaluation of this position, see *infra,* p. 57.

## CHAPTER II

## PUBLIC ORDER

### ARTICLE I. THE TERM IN CANONICAL LITERATURE

In the years that followed, both Suarez and Sanchez found support among canonists for their doctrines regarding the traveller and local statutes. Anacletus Reiffenstuel regarded the doctrine of Suarez as the more probable opinion, and he considered it to be one commonly accepted in his day.[1] Later, St. Alphonsus Ligouri followed the teaching of Sanchez.[2] By the nineteenth century this position was widely accepted as being more probable and more common.[3] The canonists who adopted this teaching did not add substantially to the arguments adduced by its early defenders. Some few of them, however, introduced a new term into the canonical doctrine. They designated as the public order that social condition or status which the superior has to maintain in order to protect the community. Thus the preservation of the public order is the special necessity that warrants the extension of the bishop's jurisdiction to include the traveller.

Perhaps the earliest use of the term in canonical literature occurs in a work of Philippus De Angelis (1824-1881). He wrote that the traveller is not bound by local statutes because he is not a subject, unless the laws are made to insure the security of the place, for it is the superior's duty to see that the public order suffers no harm, or unless the natural law intervenes in respect to the avoidance of scandal.[4]

[1] *Theologia Moralis*, I, tractatus II, disputatio III, quaestio III, n. 25.

[2] *Theologia Moralis*, I, tractatus II, caput II, dubium II, n. 156.

[3] Bargilliat, *Praelectiones Iuris Canonici* (10. ed., 2 vols., Paris, 1889), I, 63; De Angelis, *Praelectiones Iuris Canonici* (5 vols. in 9, Romae—Parisiis, 1877-1891), I, 54-55; Santi, *Praelectiones Iuris Canonici* (5 vols. in 1, Ratisbonae, 1886), I, 22-23; Wernz, *Ius Decretalium* (6 vols., Romae—Prati, 1898-1914), I, 115-117.

[4] "An peregrinus teneatur legibus peculiaribus locorum, per quae peregrinatur? Et responsio est non teneri, quia non est subditus, nisi leges positae sint pro securitate locorum, quia superior debet attendere, ne ordo publicus detrimentum

De Angelis also used the term in explaining the extent to which heretics and schismatics are bound by church laws. He regarded the question as depending upon the will of the legislator, and he ventured the opinion that the Church obliges them to observe those laws that have been established to suppress abuses and to safeguard the public order and good conduct in the community. As an example he pointed to the laws determining matrimonial impediments. The Church has asserted this obligation more than once, yet she does not bind them to observe other ecclesiastical laws that directly provide for the sanctification of the individual. This would lead only to a multiplication of their sins.[5]

Other authors followed De Angelis in teaching that laws of public order oblige heretics and schismatics. Blaise Duballet (1847-1931) wrote that they are bound by ecclesiastical laws that define the faith and by disciplinary laws that treat of the public order, the honor of the Church, the conservation of the society, not however those laws established for the greater good of the faithful.[6] Clement Marc

capiat, vel nisi ratio scandali subveniat, quia tunc praeceptum est ut legis naturalis de vitando scandalo."—*Praelectiones Iuris Canonici ad Methodum Decretalium Gregorii IX Exactae*, I, titulus II, n. 13, III.

[5] "Loquendo nunc de legibus Ecclesiae, cum per Baptismum quis Ecclesiae subditus fiat, omnes baptizati per se iis tenentur, etiamsi haeretici et schismatici sint. Tota enim questio in hoc est, an velit Ecclesia eos suis legibus obligare, quos contumaces esse ex experientia cognoscit, quemadmodum sunt haeretici et schismatici, quibus si leges imponerentur, id aliud non esset nisi eorum peccata multiplicare. Et si quid in hac materia licet opinari, nostra mens est, eos maxime teneri illis legibus observandis, quae ad abusus compescendos, aut ad ordinem publicum et honestam conversationem tuendam in societate christiana latae sunt, puta leges de impedimentis matrimonii, praesertim dirimentibus, aliaeque; namque plus semel Auctoritas Ecclesiastica requisita expresse vel aequivalenter eos teneri asseruit. Si vero sermo sit de aliis legibus ecclesiasticis, quae ad sanctificationem personarum directe intendunt, eos ab Ecclesia non obligari est dicendum."—*Loc. cit.*

[6] "Les hérétiques et schismatiques, à ne considérer que le droit et à raison de leur baptême, appartiennent à la société chrétienne et sonts sujets à ses lois; mais l'Eglise a-t-elle la volonté de les obliger? Oui, s'il s'agit de définitions de foi et de règles disciplinaires qui ont trait à l'ordre public, à l'honneur de l'Eglise et à la conservation de la société; non, s'il s'agit de lois portées *pro opportunitate et meliori bono fidelium*."—*Cours Complet de Droit Canonique et de Jurisprudence Canonico-Civile*, (3 vols., Paris—Poitiers, 1898), III, n. 1268.

(1831-1887) wrote that we may presume the Church excuses heretics and schismatics from ecclesiastical laws pertaining to personal sanctification, not however those laws that have been established to wipe out abuses and protect the public order.[7] Carlo Lombardi (1858-1908) professor at the Roman Seminary, regarded heretics and schismatics as bound to observe disciplinary laws made with direct reference to the public order rather than the welfare of individuals.[8]

Like De Angelis, B. Duballet also used the term *public order* in explaining the exceptional obligation of the traveller to observe local statutes. He taught that the traveller is bound to observe those laws established to maintain order and public security.[9] In this matter he adopted the teaching of Franciscus Santi (1830-1885), to whom he expressly referred.[10] With respect to heretics and schismatics, Santi taught that they are bound to obey laws necessary for the whole community, such as dogmatic definitions and disciplinary laws that strengthen the public order, the honor of religion, and the state of society.[11]

[7] "Secus, respectu legum, quae ad compescendos abusus et ad ordinem publicum tuendum latae sunt, v.g. circa matrimonii impedimenta. Quod enim his legibus haeretici teneantur, pluries ab ecclesiastica auctoritate, explicite vel saltem implicite declaratum est."—*Institutiones Morales Alphonsianae* (2 vols., Romae, 1885), I, cap. IV, art. II, n. 198.

[8] "Haeretici et schismatici satis probabiliter ex benigna et aequabili interpretatione mentis ecclesiae non tenentur legibus disciplinaribus, quae potiusquam publicum ordinem proxime respiciant (ut est verum v.g. de legibus inducentibus impedimenta matrimonialia) bonum singulorum directe attingunt (quales sunt v.g. leges de sacro audiendo et ieiuniis servandis); si enim eos adstringere intenderet ecclesia, potestate sua non in aedificationem, sed in destructionem uti videretur . . . ."—*Iuris Canonici Privati Institutiones.* (2. ed., 2 vols., Romae, 1901), I, 31.

[9] "Les voyageurs, les errants, quoique tenus à l'observance des lois générales, ne sont pas soumis aux lois particulières des lieux qu'ils traversent, à moins de légitimes exceptions. C'est à ce titre d'exception qu'ils sont obligés à l'observance des lois locales établies pour maintien de l'ordre et de la sécurité publique."—*Ibid.*, n. 1272.

[10] "Quare peregrini et vagi in loco in quo actu degunt, tenentur observare leges locales, quae latae sunt ad tutandam securitatem et ordinem in loco."—Santi, *Praelectiones Iuris Canonici Iuxta Ordinem Decretalium Gregorii IX*, (5 vols. in 1, Ratisbonae—Neo-Eboraci—Cincinnati, 1886), I, 22-23.

[11] "Si sermo sit de legibus necessariis pro tota communitate christiana, prout sunt definitiones dogmaticae, et leges disciplinares, quae ad ordinem publicum, ad decus religionis, et ad statum societatis firmandum pertinent, tenendum est, Ec-

Other canonists used the term in explaining the obligations of the traveller. Andrew B. Meehan (1867-1932) briefly stated the traditional doctrine in its new terms. He taught that since particular laws are territorial, the subject is obliged to observe the laws of his own community while he is in the place where the laws exist. When he leaves the place, he is, no longer bound by its laws. Neither is he bound by the particular laws of the place he visits, for he is not a subject of that superior, except with regard to those laws that concern contracts and the public order.[12]

Adolph Tanquerey (1854-1932), whose textbooks have been widely used in American seminaries, associated the notions of public order and the common security. Travellers are bound to observe special laws in the locality: those pertaining to the validity of contracts, those established to safeguard the security and public order, and those that especially concern the traveller.[13]

M. Bargilliat (1853-1926) wrote a noted general text of canon law which first appeared in 1891. He revised this work several times, and it appeared in the thirty-seventh edition in 1923. Even before the promulgation of the Code of Canon Law, he had adopted the term *public order* to explain the exceptional obligations of the traveller.[14]

clesia legibus huiusmodi obligare velle etiam haereticos et schismaticos."—*Ibid.*, p. 22.

[12] "Legibus particularibus tenentur subditi illius auctoritatis a qua lex dimanat, dummodo in territorio eidem auctoritati subjecto degant. Lex enim est territorialis, et in hoc differt a praecepto. Consequitur peregrinos non obligari ad servandas leges particulares proprii domicilii, quando alibi commorantur. Neque ligantur legibus particularibus loci ubi sunt, quia non sunt subditi auctoritatis localis. Tenentur tamen legibus quae respiciunt contractus et ordinem publicum."—Meehan, *Compendium Iuris Canonici* (Roffae, 1899), p. 26. This passage from the text of the former professor of Canon Law at St. Bernard Seminary, Rochester, New York, seems to be the earliest use of the term *public order* to be found in American canonical literature.

[13] "Peregrini certo servare tenentur quasdam leges speciales locorum ubi versantur, videlicet eas quae respiciunt validitatem contractuum, aut ad communem loci securitatem et publicum ordinem latae sint, vel specialiter peregrinos spectant."—Tanquerey, *Synopsis Theologiae Moralis* (3 vols., Tornaci—Neo-Eboraci, 1902-1905), II, 163.

[14] "[Peregrini] . probabilius *directe* non tenentur legibus locorum per quae transeunt, exceptis iis legibus quae contractus respiciunt."—Cap. 20, de foro

While these authors wrote of the public order as though it were a clearly-defined canonical idea, it is true that many others in the nineteenth and early twentieth centuries treated the traveller and his obligations without using the term at all. They adhered with more or less precision to the doctrine that the traveller is subject to local statutes only by exception. Nevertheless, it seems clear that public order was in fact a term in use among canonists. While its use was not general, the term was recognized as having a rather generally accepted meaning. Authors have suggested that its origin is to be sought in the writings of the civil jurists of that time. The following article will consider this usage of the term. For the present, it is to be noted that if the term *public order* has been borrowed from another branch of juridical science, it was not taken over by the codifiers of the law but by canonists in the several decades immediately preceding the promulgation of the Code of Canon Law.

### Article II. The Term in Private International Law

The science of Private International Law may be at least the material source of the term *public order.* This is the branch of civil jurisprudence that concerns itself with conflicts of law. Since the canonists were faced with conflicts with respect to the traveller and local statutes, it is not difficult to suppose that they were familiar with the doctrines of the civil jurists. A comparison of the canonical and civil doctrines on conflict of laws should contribute to an understanding of the relationship between the two systems.

From this viewpoint Private International Law seeks to determine which one of several simultaneously valid laws is to be applied in a given case. Thus in America the study is known simply as Conflict of Laws. In other schools of legal thought it is that branch of law that has for its purpose to determine the individual's nationality, the rights enjoyed by the alien, and finally to resolve the conflicts that arise in respect to these rights.[15]

competenti [c. 20, X, *de foro competenti,* II, 2]. *Indirecte* quidem tenerentur, si leges necessariae sint ad servandum ordinem publicum, aut si ratio scandali subveniat; quia tunc ipsum ius naturale obligat."—*Praelectiones Iuris Canonici.* (10. ed., 2 vols., Parisiis, 1899), I, 63.

[15] Pillet—Niboyet, *Manuel de Droit International Privé,* (Paris, 1924), p. 1.

In order to explain simply the teachings of the various schools of Private International Law, it is necessary to bear in mind that all laws, on the basis of the place in which they apply, can be divided into two classes. Laws are territorial or extra-territorial, depending upon whether or not they have application beyond the limits of the place in which they are enacted.

Another division that figures in the solution of conflicts of laws is based upon their subject matter. Laws are said to be real or personal. A personal law is one that applies to a person or concerns his rights. The relationship that exists between the law and the person is one that prescinds from territorial limitation. A real law concerns a thing rather than a person. Because the thing is more or less permanently situated in a place, real statutes have a relationship with a definite locality.

A problem arises when one tries to relate these classifications to one another. To equate indiscriminately personal laws with those that are extra-territorial and real statutes with those that are strictly territorial gives rise to confusion that is compounded by the fact that some laws are not so conveniently classified. They are neither real nor personal. Such is the case with laws of contract, obligations, and inheritance.

The science of Private International Law seeks to classify all laws in order to insure that each one will have the application it merits. The various schools are ranged between two extremes: the principle of absolute territoriality, and the principle of absolute personality. The former principle demands that only the proper laws of each country should be applied within its borders. This resolves the conflict of laws in a radical fashion, for it removes all foreign laws from consideration. However, such a principle makes harmonious international relations impossible. The principle of absolute personality requires that the laws of each state apply to its subjects no matter where they are. The schools of conflict law try to work the two principles into a harmonious rule based upon the territorial character of the modern state, but with due regard for the personal nature of certain laws.

Efforts to develop a doctrine of conflict law begin with the postglossators of the fourteenth century. Bartolus (1314-1357) and

Baldus (1327-1400) are the most influential members of this school. The glossators had not developed a theory to solve conflicts of jurisdiction, although they adverted to the problem and offered certain practical solutions.[16] Bartolus and others considered the problem in much greater detail. They gave some principles for the solution of conflicts of law.[17]

In the judgment of Armand Lainé (1841-1908)[18] the post-glossators tried to classify each law and give it the extension its nature required. They then chose the more useful and fitting as the competent law. They did not begin with *a priori* classifications but tried to judge each law empirically. This made for a free appraisal of each law on the basis of its own nature. It was in sharp contrast with the method chosen by later jurists who began with pre-determined categories into which they tried to fit every law. The post-glossators succeeded in developing some principles of choice with which conflicts might be solved. Where no principle could be discovered, the choice depended upon personal judgment, and great diversity was found among the solutions proposed by various jurists.[19]

An important development in the doctrine of conflict law was the rise of the French School of the sixteenth century. Bertrand D'Argentré (1519-1590) and Charles Dumoulin (1500-1566) were its founders. D'Argentré made a two-fold classification into which he divided all laws. Laws are real that have things for their object; personal if their object is a person. Certain statutes are mixed, for

[16] Thus Aldricus (1154-1171) had taught: "Sed quaeritur si homines diversarum provinciarum quae diversas habent consuetudines sub eodem iudice litigant, utrum earum iudex qui iudicandum suscepit sequi debeat? Respondeo, eam quae potior et utilior videtur debet enim iudicare."—Neumeyer, *Die gemeinrechtliche Entwickelung des internationalen Privat—und Strafrechts bis Bartolus* (2 vols., München, 1901-1916), II, 66-67. Accursius (1182-1263) stated a principle of judicial jurisdiction: "Argumentum, quod si Bononiensis Mutinae conveniatur non debet iudicari secundum statuta Mutinae quibus non subest, cum dicat quos nostrae Clementiae regit imperium."—Glossa ordinaria ad C. (1,4) 1, s. v. *quos*.

[17] Bartolus took as his point of departure the gloss of Accursius and went on to discuss contracts, delicts, trials, and testaments. See his commentary on C. (1,4) 1, reported in part below, p. 34, n. 45.

[18] *Introduction au Droit International Privé* (2 vols., Paris, 1888).

[19] Cf. Lainé, *op. cit.*, I, 93; Pillet—Niboyet, *ibid.*, p. 339.

they touch both persons and things.[20] D'Argentré regarded mixed statutes as equivalently real. He taught that in principle laws are territorial. That is to say, they apply to all persons within the territory and to none outside its borders. The only statutes that are extraterritorial are strictly personal laws. Except in the case of personal laws, each individual is subject to the laws in force in the place where he happens to be.[21]

While the application of the personal law beyond the territorial limits of the legislator's jurisdiction is an exception to the rule, it is an obligation based upon justice. This is not merely an act of courtesy whereby one country recognizes the laws of the other. The law itself demands such recognition. This is a doctrine characteristic of the French school.[22]

D'Argentré's teachings gave the impetus to the development of the Dutch School of the seventeenth century. Paulus Voet (1619-1667), Jan Voet (1647-1713), and Ulrich Huber (1636-1694) were its leaders. They adopted the two-fold division of real and personal statutes developed by the French School, but they regarded as a contradiction the principle that one sovereign state should be under any juridic obligation to employ the laws of another state. Instead, they explained that when one country finds it useful to recognize and apply the law of another country, it acts out of international courtesy and not out of any obligation. This courtesy is based upon the interest and well-being of the state which, when necessary, applies foreign laws in order to gain equal recognition for its own laws.[23]

In the beginning of the nineteenth century three men stand out for the contributions they made to the development of Private International Law. The first of these is an American judge, Joseph Story (1779-1845). He published his study of the conflict of laws in 1834.[24] Story developed his doctrine largely on the basis of legal precedent. He cited American and English cases as well as the works of Ulrich

[20] This distinction was adopted by Froland (d. 1746), Boullenois (1680-1762), Bouhier (1673-1746), and other French jurists of the eighteenth century. Cf. Lainé, *op. cit.*, II, 94-112.

[21] Cf. Pillet—Niboyet, *ibid.*, n. 271.

[22] Cf. Pillet—Niboyet, *ibid.*, n. 273.

[23] Cf. Pillet—Niboyet, *ibid.*, n. 274.

[24] *Commentaries on the Conflict of Laws* (8. ed., Boston, 1883).

Huber, Paulus and Jan Voet, and other Dutch and French authors of the eighteenth century. Thus the Dutch School gave the basis for the Anglo-American doctrine that, in principle, all laws are territorial, that the rules of conflict law are entirely within the sphere of national law, and consequently the application of foreign law is purely a matter of comity.[25]

In 1849 Friedrich Carl Von Savigny (1779-1861) published the eighth volume of *System des heutigen Römischen Rechts* in the form of a treatise on Private International Law. He regarded the proper object of law to be the right which one person possesses in relation to another. This legal relation is a fundamental principle on which Savigny's doctrine rests. He defined it as " . . . a relation of person to person determined by a rule of law, this law assigning to each individual a sphere or territory within which his will is supreme and independent of the will of other persons."[26]

Savigny rejected Story's appeal to comity in solving conflicts of law. He maintained that the judge is bound to make use of the foreign law in deciding those cases to which it is applicable. In such instances it is the only competent law. For modern jurisprudence has gradually tended towards the recognition of complete legal equality between the citizen and the foreigner.[27] In order to give equal protection to the rights of both, it is sometimes necessary for the state to admit statutes, originally foreign, as the sources from which its own court will reach a decision concerning a certain legal relation. Such a concession among sovereign states must not be regarded as an act of generosity or arbitrary will.[28] Rather, it is a proper and progressive development of law in the direction of

[25] Cf. Wolff, *Private International Law* (London: Oxford University Press, 1945), p. 33.

[26] "Von dem nunmehr gewonnenen Standpunkt aus erscheint uns jedes einzelne Rechtsverhältniss als eine Beziehung zwischen Person und Person, durch eine Rechtsregel bestimmt. Diese Bestimmung durch eine Rechtsregel besteht aber darin, dass dem individuellen Willen ein Gebiet angewiesen ist, in welchem er unabhängig von jeden fremden Willen zu herrschen hat."—Savigny, *System des heutigen Römischen Rechts* (8 vols., Berlin, 1840-1849), I, 333.

[27] Savigny, *Private International Law* (translated by William Guthrie, Edinburgh, 1869), p. 26.

[28] Savigny, *Private International Law*, pp. 26-28.

" . . . an international common law of nations having intercourse with one another. . . ."[29]

However, the principle is limited with respect to certain laws. They are reduced to two classes: laws of a strictly positive, imperative nature; and legal institutions of one state which are not recognized by another. The former laws may rest on moral grounds. An example would be a marriage law that excludes polygamy. They may also rest on reasons of public interest. This would certainly include police regulations. These laws are inconsistent with that freedom of application that prescinds from the territorial limits of different states.[30] The latter class includes such institutions as slavery and legal death. Since they are not recognized everywhere, they are withdrawn from that community of law that exists between all states.[31]

In an effort to determine the sphere of competence of law, Savigny rejected the division of real, personal, and mixed statutes. He found this distinction to be insufficient as the basis for the solution of conflicts.[32] Instead, he tried to evaluate each legal relation. This revealed its seat or the legal territory in which it resides. It revealed also the territorial law which must be applied in every instance of conflict.[33] With respect to the capacity a person enjoys both to possess rights and to act, Savigny regarded application of the law of the person's domicile as the only possible course.[34] However, he felt that the problem becomes vastly more complex when the person enters other legal relations. Thus he examined in turn personal status, the law of things, the law of obligations, succession, the law of the family, and the form of juridic acts.[35] His purpose was to determine the seat of every legal relation and the competent law by which it must be regulated.

The third man of the nineteenth century to exert a great influence on the doctrines of conflict of law was Pasquale Stanislao Mancini

[29] Savigny, *op. cit.*, p. 27.
[30] Savigny, *op. cit.*, pp. 34-36.
[31] Savigny, *op. cit.*, pp. 36-38.
[32] Savigny, *op. cit.*, pp. 97-98.
[33] Savigny, *op. cit.*, p. 96.
[34] Savigny, *op. cit.*, pp. 104-128.
[35] Savigny, *op. cit.*, pp. 104-276.

(1817-1888). In 1851 he delivered an address at the University of Turin that is considered to be the foundation of the so-called Italian School of Private International Law. He proposed the theory that nationality is the basis for international law.

Mancini formulated his doctrine more completely in a report given to the Institute of International Law meeting at Geneva in 1874.[36] He pointed out that many factors contribute to form the nation. Landscape, climate, religion, customs, and traditions have a formative influence and produce a spiritual unity among the people. Each nation is a collection of men of special characteristics, aptitudes, and needs. It follows as a natural consequence that the laws of each nation are best suited to safeguard the rights of its people.[37] Even while a person travels or lives outside his own country, he has a right to the protection afforded by its laws. The problem of Private International Law is to guarantee this right. It is the duty of the state to protect the people who dwell in its territory, and the alien has the same right as the national to call for this help. The state's obligation is founded on justice and international law.[38]

[36] *De l'utilité de rendre obligatoire pour tous les États, sous la forme d'un ou de plusieurs traités internationaux, un certain nombres de règles générales du Droit international privé pour assurer la décision uniforme des conflits entre les differents législations civilles et criminelles.*—Reported in *Journal du Droit International Privé* (Paris, 1874—), I (1874), 221-239; 285-304 (hereafter cited as *JDIP*).

[37] *JDIP*, I (1874), 225-227.

[38] "Le traitement des étrangers ne peut pas dépendre de la *comitas* et de la volonté souveraine et arbitraire de chaque État. La science ne peut considérer ce traitement que comme un devoir rigoureux de justice internationale, auquel une nation ne peut pas se soustraire sans violer le droit du gens, sans rompre le lien qui unit l'éspèce humaine dans une grande communauté de droit, fondée sur la communauté et la sociabilité de la nature humaine, sans devenir membre rebelle et réfractaire de cette société universelle, que Volfius appelait *Respublica maxima gentium*. Je ne dois pas recourir à des arguments long et compliqués pour le demontrer. Chaque État est une unité morale, en ce que les individus dont il se compose sont des hommes libres, responsables et doués de droits découlant de la nature mais non d'une concession politique.

"L'État, expression de la volonté et des intérêts communs, faillirait à son but et à sa raison d'être, si au lieu de reconnaître, de respecter et de garantir les droits et les libertés inoffensives des individus, il les meconnaissait ou les limitait. Or, de même que l'individu a le droit d'exercer sa liberté tant qu'elle ne blesse

Therefore, juridic order consists in the proper balance between the rights of the individual and the laws of the state. Laws of private order are those that protect the individual. Laws of public order and those that concern the organization of the public power pertain to the sovereignty of the state.

Following the lead of Mancini, many Italian and French jurists developed a theory to solve the conflicts that arise in implementing the principle of the personality of law. André Weiss (1854-1928) is a representative exponent of the teachings of the Italian School. He stated the purpose of conflict law in these words:

> The problem for which Private International Law seeks the solution comes down to the discovery of the measure in which the rights that belong to every man, even outside the territory of his country, are compatible with those of the state on whose soil he desires to exercise them; in what measure the *personal sovereignty* of the foreign law can be reconciled with the *territorial sovereignty* of the local law?[39]

He recognized that rights come to the individual independently of the state. Civil society is meant to serve the needs of the people. It would be a reversal of the natural order of things to say that the people are intended to serve the interests of the state.

pas la liberté des autres, on reconnaît que c'est un droit vrai et parfait, non seulement vis-a-vis les autres citoyens d'un même État, mais aussi vis-a-vis du reste du genre humain, parce que la conservation et la garantie des libertés de chaque homme ne peut avoir d'autre limite rationelle que cette même protection et garantie des libertés juridiques accordées à tous les autres.

"Les lois et les codes, oeuvres faillibles et expression relatif de la vérité telle qu'elle est conçu par les législateurs des États, ne créent pas les droits et les libertés de l'homme, mais ont le devoir de les reconnaître dans leurs juste mesure, même pour les étrangers. S'ils ne le font pas, ils violent les *droits de la justice,* et en même temps le *droit de gens,* parce que chaque État a l'intérêt à assurer les droits et les libertés légitimes de ses membres, et à les faire respecter par les autres peuples."—*JDIP,* I (1874), 230-231.

[39] "Le problème dont le droit international privé poursuit la solution revient à rechercher dans quelle mesure les droits qui appartiennent à tout homme, même en dehors du territoire de sa patrie, sont compatibles avec ceux de l'État sur le sol duquel il en demande l'exercise, dans quelle mesure la *souveraineté personnelle* de la loi étrangère peut être conciliée avec la *souveraineté territorialle* de la loi locale"?—Weiss, *Traité Théorique et Practique de Droit International Privé,* (4 vols., Paris, 1892-1901), III, 61.

Furthermore, the state is primarily an association of persons. It exists in a locality, but its principal characteristic is that it consists of individuals who are its members. While one might conceive of a society existing without a territory of its own, one could not conceive of a society without the people who make it up.[40]

A further consequence of this relationship is that the laws of each nation are best suited to serve the interest of its own citizens, no matter where they are.[41] This is clearly true regarding the national, and it is true of the alien as well. A conflict arises in respect to the alien, and the jurist must determine whether it is right to apply the law of the person or of the place. In principle the person's proper law is always to be preferred, even though he be an alien.

> The law, when it governs a private interest, always has for its object the utility of the person; it can serve as a rule only for those in whose interest it was made; but in principle it must govern them in every place and in all their juridic relationships, safeguarding the exceptions or modifications which follow: a.) from the international public order; b.) from the rule *locus regit actum;* c.) from the autonomy of the will.[42]

Regarding the first exception, Weiss distinguished the internal and the international public order. The former extends to all nationals in such a way as to require that they submit without exception to the authority of the ruler. Laws that flow from the internal public order impose an absolute obligation upon nationals and exclude the liberty accorded by the rule *locus regit actum* and the autonomy of the will.

International public order extends to aliens as well as nationals.

[40] Weiss, *ibid.*, p. 63. Compare Pacelli, *La Territorialité et Personalité Des Lois Particulièrement Dans Le Droit Canon* (Rome: Scientia Catholica, 1945), pp. 11-12. The author points out that territory is not essential to an ecclesiastical society nor to the exercise of legislative power in the Church.

[41] Weiss, *ibid.*, p. 64.

[42] " La loi, lorsqu'elle statue sur un intérêt privé, a toujours pour objet l'utilité de la personne; elle ne peut régir que ceux pour qui elle a été faite; mais ceux-là, elle doit en principe les régir en tous lieux et dans tous leurs rapports juridiques, saufs les exceptions ou atténuations qui résultent: a.) de l'ordre public international; b.) de la règle, 'locus regit actum'; c.) de l'autonomie de la volonté."—Weiss, *ibid.*, p. 68.

It requires that everyone, regardless of his nationality, should conform to certain laws because the general welfare demands this.[43]

Thus both internal and international public order have the general interest in view. The former is broader in scope and includes the latter. Internal public order concerns those matters that are necessary or useful to the state. International public order includes only that which is necessary to the state. Laws that concern internal public order impose an obligation upon all nationals. Laws that concern international public order oblige aliens as well as nationals. These laws can never be put aside, even by the rules of Private International Law.[44]

The second exception is the principle *locus regit actum*. According to this rule, the local law governs external formalities of juridic acts. The axiom has long been accepted and is confirmed by wide use. It is generally attributed to the post-glossators.[45]

Weiss investigated the juridic foundation of the axiom. It is an exception to the rule that the law of the person should apply to him wherever he may be. The source of its authority is not to be attributed to the consent of the contracting parties, for this can merely be conjectured. It does not lie in agreement among nations, for this consent cannot create such a right. Neither is the matter one of public order, for it is of no concern to the state whether one choses this or that form for his juridic acts.[46] Rather, the rule has a two-fold basis

[43] Weiss, *ibid.*, pp. 85-86.

[44] Weiss, *ibid.*, pp. 87-88.

[45] "Nunc veniamus ad glossam quae dicit quod si Bononiensis, etc. [ed. reads: 'quod si bona. et bon., etc.'] Et primo quaero quid de contractibus. Pone contractum celebratum per aliquem contrahentis. cuius loci statuta debent servari, vel spectari, quia illae quaestiones sunt multum revolutae, omissis aliis distinctionibus plenius quam Doctores dicant hic, distingue. Aut loquimur de statuto, aut de consuetudine, quae respiciunt ipsius contractus solemnitatem, aut litis ordinationem, aut de his quae pertinent ad jurisdictionem ex ipso contractu evenientis executionis. Primo casu inspicitur locus contractus et intelligo locus contractus, ubi est celebratus contractus, non de loco in quem collata est solutio."—Bartolus de Saxoferrato, *Opera Omnia* (11 vols., Venetiis, 1590-1595), VII (*In Primam Codicis Partem Commentaria*). ad C. (1,4), nn. 13-16. Cf. Weiss, *ibid.*, p. 96, n. 3.

[46] "Il est assez indifferent, au point de vue de notre ordre public, qu'un étranger fasse son testament dans telle forme ou dans telle autre, surtout si son avoir se trouve en pays étranger."—Weiss. *ibid.*, pp. 102-103.

for its authority. The first reason is a theoretic one. It is natural that formalities should be specified by local law. The second reason is a practical one. It is to the advantage of the alien that he should have the right to use the formalities specified by the law of the place in which he performs a juridic act.[47]

The third exception to the rule is the autonomy of the will. Weiss distinguishes laws that impose a strict obligation upon the subject and those that are merely facultative. "[The former] are those imperative or prohibitive laws that govern his status, his capacity, his family relationships, and in general all those matters that have the character of public order. . . . The others have for their object only to supplement his will, to interpret it, to trace the limits within which he can exercise it: but except for the case in which the public order is involved, they impose no obligation; they are facultative . . . ."[48] Thus a person voluntarily submits to these laws by acquiring property and other real rights, or by entering into a contractual relationship. Even though he does not advert to the legal implications of his act, it is presumed that he intends to abide by them, unless his contrary intention is clear.[49]

In brief, Weiss explained the theory of conflict law in this way:

> To sum up in a few words the theoretic principle which, it appears to us, must be applied to the solution of conflicts of laws, we say that every law, whether it looks exclusively to the person considered in himself, or directs him in relation with his family, his movable and immovable goods, is a *personal* law, acknowledged in principle to be extra-territorial; and that this rule is limited only, on the one hand, in the interest of the state in whose territory the application of the foreign law is demanded, that is to say, in *the international public order,* and on the other

[47] Weiss, *ibid.*, p. 105.

[48] "Ce sont les lois impératives ou prohibitives qui gouvernent son état, sa capacité, ses relations de famille, et d'une manière générale toutes celles qui ont un charactére d'ordre public . . . . D'autres n'ont pour objet que de suppléer sa volonté, de l'interpréter, de lui tracer les limites dans lesquelles elle peut s'exercer: mais sauf le cas où l'ordre public est interessé à leur stricte application, elles n'obligent pas; ce sont facultatives . . . ."—Weiss, *ibid.*, p. 112.

[49] Savigny objected to the obscure term "autonomy" and explained that the *national Law,* pp. 91-92.
person becomes subject to these laws by voluntary submission. Cf. *Private Inter-*

hand, in the private interest of the alien himself, who finds his formula in the rule *locus regit actum,* and in the autonomy of the will.[50]

Weiss related in substance the doctrine of the Italian School of Private International Law, and he is regarded as one of its leading exponents. However, his two-fold distinction of internal and international public order is not universally held by those who are associated with this school.

Thus Antoine Pillet (1857-1926) points out that there is really only one species of public order.[51] The reason is that the same factor of public necessity requires the uniform observance of every law by nationals, described by Weiss as internal public order, and of local law by the alien, called by Weiss international public order. He explains:

> . . . . it is impossible to conceive of two different public orders. What, exactly, is public order? It is the order in the state, that is to say, a certain arrangement of diverse social forces, an arrangement that is regular, normal, lasting, and planned in such a way that each one might see his essential rights respected and might develop in complete security and freedom his physical and intellectual faculties. More briefly, it is the application of certain rules indispensable to the conservation of the state.[52]

[50] "Pour résumer en quelques mots les principes théoriques qui nous paraissent devoir être appliqués à la solution des confiits des lois, nous dirons que toute loi, soit qu'elle vise exclusivement la personne considérée en elle-même, soit qu'elle la régisse dans ses rapports avec sa famille, avec ses biens, meubles ou immeubles, est une loi *personnelle,* admise en principe à l'extra-territorialité; et que cette règle ne recontre des limites que d'une part dans l'intérêt de l'État sur le territoire duquel l'application d'une loi étrangère est demandée, c'est à dire dans *l'ordre public international,* de l'autre part dans l'intérêt privé de l'étranger lui-même, qui trouve sa formule dans la régle *Locus regit actum* et dans l'autonomie de la volonté."—Weiss, *ibid.,* pp. 115-116.

[51] *De l'Ordre Public en Droit International Privé,* (Grenoble—Paris, 1890), p. 30.

[52] ". . . il est impossible de concevoir deux ordres publics differents. Qu'est-ce que l'ordre public en définitive? C'est l'ordre dans l'État, c'est-à-dire un certain arrangement des diverses forces sociales, arrangement régulier, normal, durable, et combiné, de telle façon que chacun voie ses droits essentiels respectés et puisse développer en toute sécurité et en toute liberté ses facultés tant physiques qu'in-

Pillet indicated that while the matter of public order appears to be one of the most important points of international law, it is one concerning which there are great diversities of opinion. However, there are certain points upon which all agree. Thus, whether by comity or by right, no foreign law can be applied in such a way as to imperil the vital interests of the state.[53] The legislator has a twofold obligation. He must protect the state and the interests of its citizens.[54] Laws that serve either of these purposes are in the public interest. Some are essential to the state; others are merely useful. Laws that are essential to the state are those that safeguard its existence or provide that it will continue to exist in its present form. Laws that protect the citizen and his rights are useful to the state as well.

Pillet indicated the laws that he regarded as essential for the conservation of the state. First there are those laws that concern its political and administrative organization. Thus police regulations evidently concern the public order.[55] Then he regarded all penal laws to be essential, for the state can maintain order only by punishing the crimes of the alien in the same way as it punishes those of the national.[56] As to civil laws, he considered that the public order is affected only by those laws, the absence of which would, by its nature, bring on the dissolution of the society.[57] This danger could be in the material, moral, or economic order, but it must be a real threat to the society.

Pillet emphasized the exceptional character of public order. The liberty of the individual is the rule, and its limitation in the name of public order is the exception. It requires the suspension of ordinary principles of jurisprudence, and it must be interpreted strictly.[58]

tellectuelles. Plus brèvement, c'est l'application de certaines règles indispensables à la conservation de l'État."—Pillet, *ibid.*, p. 37.

[53] *Ibid.*, p. 2.

[54] *Ibid.*, p. 3.

[55] *Ibid.*, p. 18.

[56] *Ibid.*, p. 19.

[57] "C'est une raison suffisante de nous en tenir à la seule idée de la conservation sociale et de ne réputer d'ordre public que les seules dispositions légales dont l'absence paraîtrait de nature à entraîner la dissolution de notre état social."—*Ibid.*, p. 20.

[58] *Ibid.*, p. 17.

> In other words, it will not suffice that a law conforms to the public order, or even [that it is] suited to its preservation, for it really to be of public order; it will be necessary that it be indispensable to the public order, that the absence of its provisions has for its result the destruction of the public order.[59]

Further, the public order is not to be confused with the interest of the citizens, for the alien has the same rights and enjoys equality with the national. The ruler is not to favor one over the other.[60]

In short, laws of public order are those that are essential to the existence and functioning of the state. The legislator or the judge who extends this notion sanctions an injustice for he deprives the alien of his right.[61]

On the basis of this short summary of the development of Private International Law it is apparent that the doctrines proposed by the various schools were of great interest to jurists of the nineteenth and the early twentieth centuries. However great their differences, all agreed that no state must apply a foreign law at the expense of its own security, for the ruler's duty is to protect both the citizens and the society entrusted to his care. The term *public order* was applied by Italian and French jurists to those local laws that, by way of exception, are extended to include aliens as well as nationals for the protection of the state.

These juridic notions were current in the nineteenth century. Indeed, the term *public order* passed into canonical usage. Canonists immediately prior to the preparation of the Code of Canon Law introduced this term into their consideration of the subject of law. They did not use it as a means of introducing a new doctrine. There is no evidence that they made any effort to apply it in other than the traditional frame of reference. Instead, it would seem that they chose this term because it suited the canonical doctrine as it was then understood. They used it to explain the exceptional obligation of the traveller to observe local statutes, or to explain the extent to which

[59] "En d'autres termes, il ne suffira pas qu'une loi soit conforme à l'ordre public, ou même propre à assurer son maintien, pour qu'elle soit réellement d'ordre public; il faudra qu'elle soit indispensable à cet ordre public, que l'absence de ses dispositions ait pour résultat de détruire l'ordre public."—*Ibid.*, p. 18.

[60] *Ibid.*, p. 25.

[61] *Ibid.*, p. 27.

they considered heretics and schismatics to be bound by the Church's law.

Therefore, the use of the term *public order* in the Code of Canon Law is not an evidence of change in juridical principles. The codifiers chose a term that was current in juridical studies and suited the traditional doctrine, a term that had already crept into canonical literature. The term itself, but not necessarily its meaning, seems to have been derived from the doctrines of Private International Law.

## Article III. The Meaning of Public Order

### A. The Norm for Interpreting Public Order in the Church

The notion of public order is a familiar one to civil jurists, for it is fundamental to the resolution of conflicts of law. The term developed among the Italian and French jurists. The concept is recognized in German law, and it appears in English and American legal writing as the public policy exception.[62] Notwithstanding differences of terminology, the idea appears in all schools of conflict law that the state must protect its vital interests. This is a principle rooted in the nature of society. It is analogous to the individual's right of self-defence. In the sphere of conflict law the principle limits the extent to which the state will exempt the alien from subjection to its laws.

The canonist is concerned with a similar problem in reference to the traveller and local statutes. The glossators made reference to it. The earliest decretists regarded the traveller to be subject to all local laws.[63] Later Suarez defended this doctrine and developed juridic principles as its basis.[64]

The later decretists and the decretalists taught that the traveller is free in principle from subjection to local statutes. He is bound to observe them in exceptional cases.[65] Sanchez regarded this doc-

[62] Cf. Bodenheimer, "The Public Policy Exception in Private International Law: A Reappraisal in the Light of Legal Philosophy,"—*Seminar* (Washington, D.C.: The School of Canon Law, The Catholic University of America, 1943-1956), XII (1954), 51-66.

[63] Cf. Onclin, *De territoriali vel personali legis indole* (Gemblaci: J. Duculot, 1938), p. 24 (hereafter cited as *De Legis Indole*).

[64] Cf. *supra*, pp. 1-7.

[65] Cf. Onclin, *op. cit.*, p. 31.

trine to be more probable.[66] He and others developed the juridic reasoning that serves as its foundation. They did not simply repeat the sources of exceptional jurisdiction proposed by the glossators. Instead, they sought to determine the foundation for these norms. They taught that the ruler's exceptional jurisdiction over the traveller is founded upon the special need to protect the community from harm. This harm may be spiritual[67] or material.[68] But its common note is the threat posed to the society.[69]

The later canonists of both schools agreed that public necessity is the basis for the ruler's extended jurisdiction. Both the followers of Suarez, who taught that this urgency is present in every case, and those who subscribed to Sanchez' doctrine that only exceptional cases are of such vital necessity, taught that the ruler has the duty and the power to protect the community from harm. This is the reason for his jurisdiction over the traveller.

In the late nineteenth century some canonists introduced into their discussion of the traveller's subjection to local statutes the notion of public order.[70] Philippus De Angelis and Franciscus Santi expressed themselves with notable clarity. Both taught that the traveller is subject to local laws only in special cases. This had then become the common doctrine. De Angelis explained that the traveller is not obliged to obey local statutes *"nisi leges positae sint pro securitate locorum, quia superior debet attendere, ne ordo publicus detrimentum capiat. . . ."*[71] Santi wrote that the traveller must obey laws *"quae latae sunt ad tutandam securitatem et ordinem in loco."*[72]

The present law gives full juridic force to the doctrine of Sanchez and his followers and defines the traveller's obligation in the frame of reference of public order and the solemnities of acts. It seems

[66] Cf. *supra*, pp. 7-10.

[67] Cf. Suarez, *De Virtute Religionis*, tract. II, lib. II, c. XIV, n. 11 (reported above, p. 5, n. 28).

[68] Cf. Ferraris, *Prompta Bibliotheca*, V, verbo *Lex*, art. III, n. 45 (reported above, p .13, n. 58).

[69] Cf. *supra*, p. 20.

[70] Cf. *supra*, pp. 21-25.

[71] *Praelectiones Iuris Canonici*, I, titulus II, n. 13, III (reported above, p. 21, n. 4).

[72] *Praelectiones Iuris Canonici*, I, 22-23 (reported above, p. 23, n. 10).

clear that in using the former term the legislator has chosen a comparatively new phrase. However, the traveller's obligation remains unchanged. This aspect of the present law retains the doctrine that had been commonly accepted prior to the promulgation of the Code of Canon Law. Consequently, the new law must be understood in the light of the old.[73] The notion of public order must be explained with reference to previous canonical jurisprudence.

### B. The Concept of Public Order in the Church

Order is the relationship[74] of diverse elements working towards a goal.[75] The laws of each society specify the way in which its members are to co-operate to attain their common goal. Law establishes a pattern of relationships involving the members of the society with respect to each other and with respect to the community. Conformity to this pattern is social order.

Public order is conformity to laws that have a special urgency. It is observance of a pattern of conduct that is vital to the community. This is clearly the sense in which the legislator uses the term to indicate that the traveller must obey local statutes *that secure public order*.[76] Properly speaking, public order is a pattern of behavior in the community. It can also be regarded as the basis for a classification of law. There are laws that secure public order and laws that do not. The nature of each is seen in the purpose to which it is directed. In itself, however, public order is nothing else than conformity to the requirements of such a law. When these requirements are flaunted, the public order is disturbed. When they are obeyed, the public order is made secure.

[73] Can. 6, 2°-3°

[74] " . . ordo semper dicitur per comparationem ad aliquod principium."—S. Thomas de Aquino, *Summa Theologiae* (Pars Prima et Prima Secundae, cura et studio Sac. Petri Caramello, Taurini—Romae: Marietti, 1950), I, q. 42, a. 3 c.

[75] "Invenitur autem duplex ordo in rebus. Unus quidem partium alicuius totius seu alicuius multitudinis ad invicem, sicut partes domus ad invicem ordinantur. Alius est ordo rerum in finem. Et hic ordo est principalior, quia primus . ."—S. Thomas de Aquino, *Commentarium in Decem Libros Ethicorum* (Parisiis, 1875), I, 1, 1. ". . . ad ordinem tria concurrunt, primo quidem distinctio cum convenientia, secundo cooperatio, tertio finis."—S. Thomas de Aquino, *Commentarium in De Divinis Nominibus* (Parisiis, 1889), c. IV, lect. 1.

[76] " . . . [legibus] quae ordini publico consulunt . "—Can. 14, § 1, 2°

Thus conformity to law makes for order in the community. The distinctive characteristic of public order is the element of social necessity. It has to do with the protection of society as it exists here and now. Public order, therefore, is conformity to those laws that are necessary for the security of the society. This is clear from a consideration of the laws that define this order and afford it protection. The note whereby they are distinguished from all other laws indicates the formality under which public order is to be distinguished from other patterns of conduct in the community.

St. Isidore of Seville (*c.* 560-636) listed as one of the qualities of every law that it must be useful to the citizens.[77] In the classic definition of law, its object must be the common good.[78]

Suarez distinguished the matter of the common good. The object of a law can be the common good itself, as some good that does not belong to any individual but is to the advantage of all. Its object can also be the good that belongs to an individual but in a secondary way benefits the entire community.[79] In every case, however, the law serves the interest of the persons who make up the society rather than that of the community considered in an abstract fashion, as though it were something existing apart from its members.[80]

[77] "Erit enim lex honesta, iusta, . nullo privato commodo, sed communi utilitate civium conscripta."—*Etymologiae,* V, c. 21—Cf. c. 2, D. IV.

[78] "[Lex est] . . . quaedam rationis ordinatio ad bonum commune, ab eo qui curam communitatis habet, promulgata."—*Summa Theologiae,* I-IIae, q. 90, a. 4 c.

[79] ". . . unum est, quod per se primo commune est, quia non est sub alicuius privati dominio, sed totius communitatis, ad cuius usum vel usum fructum immediate ordinatur: huiusmodi sunt templa, vel res sacrae, magistratus, pascua communia, seu prata et similia . . . Aliud vero est bonum commune solum secundario et quasi per redundantiam; immediate autem bonum privatum est, quia sub dominio privatae personae, et ad eius commodum proxime ordinatur: dicitur autem etiam commune . . ."—*De Legibus,* I, 7, 7. "Nam quaenam leges proxime versantur circa materiam communem, aliae circa bona singulorum: semper tamen ratio propter quam lex versatur circa utramque materiam est commune bonum, quod propterea debet esse primario intentum."—*Ibid,* n. 8.

[80] "Non est bonum societatis abstracte sumptae, quasi haec esset ens per se subsistens prout a membris distinguitur, sed est bonum omnium communitatis membrorum. Hoc autem bonum commune ultimo est beatitudo, quod est bonum commune omnium hominum, et immediate sed in ordine ad beatitudinem etiam

Michiels (1890-) indicates that the good towards which a law is directed is generally regarded to be a social and public good. This is true when the direct and total object of a law is primarily common to everyone. It is not proper to individuals but is to the advantage of the entire community. Thus laws governing ecclesiastical elections concern the individual only in a secondary way. Primarily they are to the advantage of the society itself. The good they seek is social. It is the public good.

It is also possible for a law to have the public good for its object only in an indirect way. In this case the direct object of the law is a good that is proper to the individual. The law is to the advantage of the person, but the good which is its object belongs also to many individuals. It is protected by a rule that is common to all of them. The direct object of the law is the individual good. Inasmuch as it is proper to many, this good is common. In a secondary way the law affects the community, for it is in the interest of all that this common good should be protected. Thus laws that are primarily to the advantage of a class, such as the clergy, pastors, religious, are to the advantage of the community in a secondary way.[81]

However, the distinction must be applied with due regard for the diverse ends of the civil and ecclesiastical societies. The state directs its activity to the preservation of the public good and provides for the temporal welfare of its citizens inasmuch as they are members

felicitas temporalis."—Brys, *Tractatus de Legibus* (Brugis: apud Editiones Car. Beyaert, 1942), pp. 4-5.

[81] "Quando de legibus dicitur eas essentialiter ordinari ad bonum commune, *generatim intelligitur* eas necessario intendere *bonum* communitatis ecclesiasticae *sociale publicum,* seu eiusdem communitatis ordinem externum, communitati secundum se, qua tali, proprium: *sive directe et totaliter,* quatenus versantur circa objectum quod per se et primarie omnibus commune est, non in unius alteriusve privato dominio constitutum, quodque proinde immediate communitati prodest, licet postea in bonum privatum redundet; tales sunt v.g. leges circa electionem praelatorum conditae; *sive indirecte et distributive,* quatenus objectum legis primo et per se est aliquid privatum, in privato dominio singulorum membrorum constitutum, particulare membrorum commodum promovere natum, quod tamen per redundationem quamdam, est toti societati commune, in quantum commodum illorum singulorum est, ex ipso operis fine, ad bonum totius communitatis ordinatum. "—Michiels, *Normae Generales Juris Canonici* (2. ed., 2 vols., Parisiis—Tornaci—Romae: Desclée et Socii, 1949), I, 174-175 (hereafter cited as *Normae Generales*).

of the community.[82] The Church has a divine mandate to provide both for the spiritual welfare of the ecclesiastical society and the sanctification of the individual soul.

With regard to the Church, Michiels points out that many of her laws, and especially those that are disciplinary in character, have the public good as their direct object. Others, and especially moral laws, directly and immediately concern the spiritual welfare of the individual.[83]

In order to explain this, it is important to note that the common good embraces both the public good and the private good to the extent that this contributes to the public good. What is opposed to the public good is not the private good but the singular good (*bonum singulare*), for this has reference to the individual alone. It does not contribute, even indirectly, to the public good. It is therefore excluded from the sphere of the common good.

We may say in respect to the object of law that there are two goods that are mutually exclusive, the common good and the singular good. The latter can never be the object of a law, for it does not in any way contribute to the advantage of the community.[84] The common good includes within its scope the public good and the private good to the extent that the latter contributes to the public good.

Every law has the common good for its object. Certain laws are directed to the public good, for they concern the welfare of the com-

[82] "Addo tertio potestatem civilem legislativam, etiam in pura natura spectatam, non habere pro fine intrinsico et per se intento felicitatem naturalem vitae futurae: immo nec propriam felicitatem naturalem vitae praesentis, quatenus ad singulos homines, ut particulares personae sunt, pertinere potest, sed eius finem esse felicitatem naturalem communitatis humanae perfectae, cuius curam gerit, et singulorum hominum, ut sunt membra talis communitatis, ut in ea scil. in pace et iustitia vivant et cum sufficientia bonorum, quae ad vitae corporalis conservationem et commoditatem spectant, et cum ea probitate morum, quae ad hanc externam pacem et felicitatem reipublicae et convenientem humanae naturae conservationem necessaria est."—Suarez, *De Legibus*, III, 11, 7.

[83] *Normae Generales*, I, 175. Pio Fedele (1911—) suggests that canon law as a whole is directed ultimately to the salvation of souls. He regards this as a public good with respect to the ecclesiastical society, and he concludes that all her laws are laws of public order. Cf. *Discorso Generale sull'Ordinamento Canonico* (Padova: Casa Editrice Dottor Antonio Milan, 1941), pp. 131-136.

[84] Rather, the singular good may be the object of a privilege, which is a *lex privata*. Cf. c. 3, D. III.

munity as such. Only indirectly do they confer an advantage upon the individual. Laws that secure the public order fall within this category. They have as their direct object the protection of the community. However, the public good and the public order are not synonymous. While they have this note in common that they serve the interest of the community directly, they are not coextensive. Every law that secures the public order has for its object a public good. The reverse is not true. The domain of public order is more restricted than that of the public good.

There are two principal opinions concerning the formal element that distinguishes the public order and the public good. One opinion is offered by LePicard (1878-1948). He suggests that the public order is determined and protected by fixed rules and principles. The public order is disturbed only upon violation of one of these rules. However, the public good can be harmed as a result of special circumstances. Le Picard bases this distinction on canon 1586.[85] The canon provides that the promotor of justice must be cited to take part in contentious causes in which the ordinary judges that the public good is in peril. Le Picard concludes that judgment is reserved to the ordinary because special circumstances enter in to jeopardize the public good. By reason of his office the ordinary is the one best equipped to evaluate these circumstances. Therefore he, not the judge, is to decide whether the promotor of justice must be summoned.[86]

Le Picard takes this canon as the source of the criterion with which public order and public good must be distinguished. He concludes that the public order is something constant. It is determined by rules that do not change. If the notion seems to be uncertain, the reason is that the legislator did not enumerate the rules whereby public order is determined and protected. If it varies in different periods and localities, the reason is that men are not always and everywhere

[85] "Constituatur in dioecesi *promotor iustitiae* et *defensor vinculi;* ille pro causis, tum contentiosis in quibus bonum publicum, Ordinarii iudicio, in discrimen vocari potest, tum criminalibus; iste pro causis, in quibus agitur de vinculo sacrae ordinationis aut matrimonii."

[86] Le Picard, "La Notion d'Ordre Public en Droit Canonique"—*Nouvelle Revue Théologique* (Paris, 1869-) LV (1928), 366-376 (hereafter cited as *NRT*).

the same.[87] Thus the public order depends upon time, place, and social milieu. At any given moment of space and time it is constant and stable.[88]

On the contrary, the public good depends upon special circumstances. They vary in each case. Thus the dignity of the person concerned, the notoriety that is associated with the particular action, the scandal that it causes, and similar circumstances might involve the public good in a contentious cause that, of itself, is the adjudication of private rights. Since these conditions are so closely associated with the special characteristics of the locality, their evaluation is reserved to the local ordinary. The tenor of canon 1586 suggests that he is best qualified to judge them.

Le Picard offers a carefully reasoned explanation of the distinction between public order and public good. He first defines the common good as that which is useful to the society. He refers to St. Isidore of Seville, whose statement that the law must be of common utility to the citizens is a fundamental legal concept.[89] Since he regards the common good as that which is useful to society, Le Picard maintains that the public good is that which is necessary.[90] The public order also has the element of social necessity. He feels that the formality under which the two are to be distinguished is suggested in canon 1586. The public order is stable and unchanging, for it depends upon certain laws that define its scope and afford it protection. When one of these laws is violated, the public order is disturbed. A danger to the public good arises, not simply from the violation of a law, but by reason of other factors for which the law made no provision. It pertains to the local ordinary to judge whether

[87] *Ibid.*, p. 364.

[88] *Ibid.*, p. 366.

[89] "Il semble que le bien commun, objet de toute loi, comprenne toute ce qui est utile même indirectement ou secondairement à la collectivité .”—*Dictionnaire de Droit Canonique* (Paris: Letouzey et Ané, 1924—), II, col. 828, s.v. *Bien public, bien privé* (hereafter cited as *DDC*). Cf. c. 2, D. IV, and *supra*, p. 42.

[90] "Le bien public, auquel se réfèrent seules certaines lois et qui a par conséquent une moindre extension que le bien commun, paraît se restreindre à ce qui est nécessaire à la collectivité, à ce dont elle ne pourrait être privée sans un dommage positif."—*DDC*, II, col. 828.

special circumstances are present whereby the illicit act involves the public good. This may be the case even though the law that is transgressed is not one intended to secure public order. Thus when an illicit act endangers the community, not precisely by reason of the law that is broken, but by reason of circumstances that the legislator did not foresee, such an act affects the public good but not the public order.[91]

Van Hove (1872-1947) offers another opinion. He maintains that certain laws have in view the protection of the public good. It is in peril only when one of these laws is transgressed. The sense of canon 1586 is that the local ordinary must judge whether the violation of a law that has the public good for its object is actually involved in a contentious cause before his tribunal. His judgment is directed to the cause at hand. The public good is threatened only if a law has been violated that serves to defend it. It pertains to the ordinary to determine whether the violation of such a law is pertinent to an otherwise private controversy that has been brought before the court.[92]

As a consequence canon 1586 cannot supply the norm for distinguishing the public good and the public order. The difference lies rather in the measure of social necessity that each implies. The public order is absolutely necessary for the security of the society. Laws that defend the public order are so vital to the society that everyone must conform to them. Therefore they bind the traveller although he is ordinarily free from subjection to local statutes.[93]

Of the two opinions that of Van Hove seems to be the true one. He arrives at a notion of public order that is in accord with traditional jurisprudence. For the term first entered into canonical

[91] Le Picard, *La Communauté de la Vie Conjugale* (Paris: Librairie du Receuil Sirey, 1930), p. 30.

[92] "Arguit [Le Picard] ex canone 1586 quo iudicio Ordinarii committitur, an promotor iustitiae intervenire debeat in causis contentiosis, in quibus bonum publicum in discrimen vocari potest. Ni fallimur, bonum publicum in discrimen vocari non potest, nisi propter violatam legem quae versatur circa bonum publicum. Iudicio autem Ordinarii committitur an violatio legis huiusmodi sit conexa vel non causae mere contentiosae, in qua agitur de iuribus privatorum." —Van Hove, *Commentarium Lovaniense*, Volumen I, Tomus II (*De Legibus Ecclesiasticis*, Mechliniae—Rome: H. Dessain, 1930), p. 223.

[93] *Loc. cit.*

literature in the nineteenth century as an explanation of the traveller's subjection to local statutes. The obligation of the traveller with respect to public order is unchanged in the Code of Canon Law. According to the norm of canon 6 the old law is the guide for a proper understanding of the present use of this term. The distinctive note of the old law was that the traveller must observe those statutes that protect the public security. Van Hove rightly points to this element as the formality under which the distinction between public order and the public good must be made.

With this in mind it will be helpful to recall that every law must in some way be directed to the common good. Some laws are directly concerned with the public good. They are primarily in the interest of the society, and only in a secondary way do they affect its members. Other laws are directly concerned with the private good, the interest of the members of the society, but only inasmuch as this contributes to the public good.

In either case, the subject is bound to obey the law to the extent that it is imposed upon him. His obligation arises from the fact of his membership in the community. He must contribute his share to the welfare of the society and its members. He enjoys in return certain advantages that follow from his membership.

The traveller does not belong to the community. His domicile is elsewhere, and ordinarily his subjection is to the laws of his own superior. His conduct is usually in the interest of his own community. As a rule the traveller is not bound to contribute to the welfare of another community, but he cannot inflict harm upon it.[94] The community has the right to protect itself. Certain of its laws, those that are vital to its security, oblige the traveller like the resident. If he should disobey them, he would harm the community just as much as would one of its members. These are laws that secure public order.

[94] "Dici fortasse possit ordini publico consuli per eas leges quae ad commune damnum avertendum, potiusquam ad promovendum bonum publicum latae sunt. Peregrini enim communi alieni territorii bono cooperari per se non debent, damnosi tamen esse vetantur."—Vermeersch—Creusen, *Epitome Iuris Canonici* (3 vols., Vol. I, 7. ed., 1949; Vol. II, 6. ed., 1940; Vol. III, 6. ed., 1946, Mechliniae—Romae; H. Dessain), I, 111-112.

This interpretation seems to find confirmation in a comparison of the rules set down for the Sacred Roman Rota in 1910 and the norms given in 1934. In the first document the promotor of justice is described as bound to defend the public good and order.[95] In the second document it is indicated that he must take part in criminal causes and in contentious causes in which the public good is in peril.[96] There is an evident relationship between public order and the public good. Laws that secure public order are those that are necessary to safeguard the public good. They are essential to the security of the society. Whenever anyone violates such a law, he harms society itself. Consequently these laws oblige everyone. They bind the traveller even though he is ordinarily excused from subjection to local statutes.

Public order is conformity to laws of this sort. It is a certain pattern of conduct that is essential to the security of the society in that it is indispensable to the protection of a necessary public good.

## Article IV. Comparison of the Civil and Canonical Concepts

There is good reason to believe that canonists borrowed the term *public order* from the science of Private International Law. It appears first in the writings of the Italian and French civil jurists in the late nineteenth century. Canonists of the same period, when they introduced the phrase into ecclesiastical jurisprudence, chose an expression well-suited to the principles that had already been developed in respect to the traveller and the local statute. There is a relationship between the concept found in the civil and in the canon law. Yet it seems proper to regard public order as a fully developed canonical doctrine. It was not taken over in whole cloth from the civil law. The canonist is not to turn to the civil law to find a norm for its interpretation. The ecclesiastical concept of public order is to

[95] "In causis criminalibus et in iis quae natura sua ordinem et bonum publicum respiciunt, tribunal primae instantiae, quoad ordinem stricte iudicialem, nequit repraesentari a procuratore aut advocato proprio, sed ordinem et bonum publicum defendet Promotor iustitiae apud S. Rotae tribunal."—*Regulae servandae in iudiciis apud Sacrae Romanae Rotae Tribunal,* 4 aug. 1910, § 39, 1 —*AAS,* II (1910), 798.

[96] "Promotor iustitiae intervenire debet in omnibus causis criminalibus, itemque in contentiosis in quibus bonum publicum in discrimen vocari potest, iis exceptis

be understood according to the rule of interpretation which the legislator himself has indicated.

Prior to the promulgation of the Code of Canon Law the legislator admitted use of the text of Roman law as a supplementary source of canon law.[97] This is no longer allowed. General principles of law are admitted as a supplementary source when there is no canonical prescript.[98] We are not concerned with such a case here. There is no *lacuna legis*. The legislator has given a rule. Our concern is to understand properly the idea that is presented in the law.

Furthermore, the legislator gives no reason to suppose that in the matter of public order he has taken the civil doctrine and given it canonical force. There are some instances in which the Code of Canon Law expressly adopts and makes its own a prescript of the civil law,[99] but this is not one of them.

The doctrine of the civil jurists has no place as a norm for the interpretation of public order in the Church. Canon 14 adopts the term to express a prescript that is retained from the former law. It is to be understood in accord with the law prior to 1918 and in the light of the explanations given by the approved authors frequently cited by the Holy See.[100]

There is, however, a close relationship between these concepts as they are found in civil and canon law. The writings of the civil jurists seem to be the source from which the canonists borrowed the term. The canonical doctrine is similar in many ways to that proposed by the civil jurists. While we cannot admit the civil doctrine as the norm of interpretation, it is true that a comparison of the two concepts will clarify our notion of public order in the Church.

The civil jurists agree that the characteristic note of public order is the element of social necessity.[101] Laws that protect the public

quae ad vinculi Defensorem spectant."—*Normae Sacrae Romanae Rotae Tribunalis,* 29 iunii 1934, art. 24, § 1—*AAS* XXVI (1934), 456.

[97] C. 1, D. X; c. 1, X, *de novi operis nuntiatione*, V, 32. Cf. Wernz, *Ius Decretalium*, I, 297.

[98] Can. 20.

[99] Cans. 1059; 1080; 1508; 1529.

[100] Can. 6, 2°-3°.

[101] Weiss, *Traité Théorique et Pratique de Droit International Privé,* III, 87-88; Pillet, *De l'Ordre Public en Droit International Privé*, p. 37.

order are only those that are absolutely indispensable to the society. Their violation results in the destruction of the public order.[102] These laws are essential to the conservation of the state.[103] No one can be excused from observing them. They bind the alien, although he is not ordinarily a subject.[104] For if he violates such a law, he inflicts harm upon the community just as if he were its member. The right of the community to defend itself from this harm is the source of its jurisdiction over the traveller.[105]

This jurisdiction is exceptional. In principle the alien is free from subjection to local statutes. Laws of public order are the exception to the rule. They must be interpreted strictly.[106]

The legislator who extends this notion and subjects the alien to local statutes that are not of public order does him an injustice. He deprives the alien of his right to liberty.[107]

In a similar way the canonists, at least from the sixteenth century, taught that the traveller is subject to local laws by reason of a certain social necessity. Their subjection is required for the peace and good order of the community,[108] for its protection from harm,[109] for the welfare of the society.[110] Sanchez and many others regarded this social necessity to be an exceptional occurrence. Ordinarily the community is not endangered by the conduct of the traveller. Only when this danger arises does the traveller become subject to the local statute.[111] This is the principle found in canon 14.

Thus in both the civil and ecclesiastical society the notion of public order has certain common characteristics. Its distinctive note is that it concerns the protection of the society. Its object is the

[102] Pillet, *ibid.*, p. 17.

[103] Pillet, *ibid.*, p. 37.

[104] Weiss, *ibid.*, pp. 85-86.

[105] Le Picard, *La Communauté de la Vie Conjugale*, p. 34.

[106] Pillet, *ibid.*, p. 17.

[107] Pillet, *ibid.*, p. 27.

[108] Suarez, *De Legibus*, III, c. XXXIII, n. 3.

[109] Sanchez, *De Matrimonio*, III, Disp. XVIII, n. 14.

[110] Sanchez, *ibid*, n. 16; Laymann, *Theologia Moralis*, I, tract. IV, cap. XII, n. 5, ad quintum; Schmalzgrueber, *Ius Canonicum Universum*, Tomus Primus, Pars Prima, pars I, titulus II, n. 42.

[111] Sanchez, *ibid.*, n. 6.

public security. Laws that protect the public order are only those that have for their direct object the protection of a good that is indispensable to the society as such. The society cannot permit the violation of these laws by anyone without allowing its own destruction, but such laws are the exception rather than the rule. The presumption stands that a law is not of vital necessity to the security of either society. Only a law that clearly is characterized by a social necessity is one that safeguards the public order.

This principle of social necessity that is the basis of public order is the same in both Church and state. Nevertheless, the two societies are fundamentally different. The one seeks the salvation of souls. The other seeks the temporal well-being of its members. Each society has a different end; each uses different means to attain it. Public order in the Church is not the same as it is in the state.

Even within the ecclesiastical society the public order is not the same at every time and in every place. The needs of each diocese are different. What is a matter of public order in one place need not be so in another. Otherwise the Church could have made general laws to provide for the vital needs that would arise in any part of the world. Public order often depends upon local conditions. The local superior is in the position to judge these factors. It is his duty to frame the laws that will determine and protect the public order in his place of jurisdiction.

While it helps us to compare the civil and canonical notions, we must not attempt to apply the doctrine of the civil jurists to canonical jurisprudence. Public order in the Church follows from the nature of the ecclesiastical society and is based on well-established canonical principles. It is to be understood in the frame of reference of the canon law itself. At the same time it is clear that, even within the Church, public order will vary according to circumstances of time and place. Therefore it is to be judged according to the needs of each locality. Public order in the Church has these characteristic notes. It concerns the protection of a public good that is indispensable to the ecclesiastical society. Laws that secure the ecclesiastical public order are those laws alone that require complete obedience in order to protect the society as such.

## CHAPTER III

## LAW AND PUBLIC ORDER

Public order is a pattern of conduct prescribed by law and found to be essential to the security of society in that it is indispensable for the protection of a necessary public good. Laws that have it as their direct and primary purpose to enjoin such behavior are those that secure public order.

In Church and state the underlying principle is the same, but the full significance of public order depends upon the nature of each society and upon local circumstances. A matter of public order in civil law need not be such in canon law. Similarly, the concept differs from one locality to another. The principle is the same. Its application varies.[1] The legislator presumably knows best the needs of the community. It is part of his office to judge the requirements of public order and to establish the laws needed to protect it.

### Article I. Local Statutes that Secure Public Order

In the Church public order is given its proper meaning in the frame of reference of the traveller's obligation to obey local statutes. It would be impossible to make a complete and exclusive list of such laws, but they are recognized by the purpose they serve. In identifying such statutes, it is important to bear in mind the extent of power exercised by the local ordinary. His office is carefully defined in law. He has the right and duty to govern his diocese in temporal as well as spiritual matters. He has the power to make laws, to judge, and to impose sanctions, but he must exercise this power according to the general law.[2]

The Code of Canon Law indicates those who are subject to the local ordinary. In general his subjects are determined by domicile or

[1] This causes some to regard public order as a vague and uncertain idea. Thus F. Geny, *Science et Technique en droit privé positif* (4 vols. in 8, Paris, 1914-1924), III, 482: "Ces mots sonores 'ordre public' restent à l'état d'enveloppe vide."

[2] Can. 335, § 1.

quasi-domicile.[3] The traveller is excluded. Although he is present, his domicile (quasi-domicile) is elsewhere. He is not obliged to observe local statutes unless the general law provides otherwise. The law does provide otherwise in canon 14, §1, 2°. The traveller must observe those local statutes that secure public order or determine the solemnities of acts.[4] In these two instances the traveller becomes subject to the local ordinary. Public order and the solemnities of acts become exceptional sources of jurisdiction. They are exceptions because the law states that the traveller is ordinarily considered free. They are sources of jurisdiction for the local ordinary and of subjection for the traveller.

This is the rule of general law. It obliges everywhere. Both the traveller and the local ordinary must act in conformity with it. The Church could have provided otherwise, but she has not done so. There would be nothing unreasonable about it if the Church had ruled that the traveller is subject to local statutes. She can and does provide otherwise in particular cases.[5] Contrary customs could arise in a particular locality.[6] However, the general norm of law is that the traveller is not bound to observe local statutes unless they secure the public order or determine the solemnities of acts. This rule embodies the teaching regarded as more probable by canonists before the promulgation of the Code of Canon Law.[7] It is the rule to which the traveller must look as a guide for his conduct and the norm to which the local ordinary must adapt those statutes that he wishes to extend to others besides his own subjects.

### A. Local Statutes Binding the Traveller by Reason of General Law

By force of general law the Church obliges the traveller to conform to certain local statutes. This does not mean that these laws secure public order.[8] There is no intrinsic necessity that demands

[3] Can. 13, § 2.

[4] "Peregrini [non adstringuntur] . . . legibus territorii in quo versantur, iis exceptis quae ordini publico consulunt, vel actuum solemnia determinant . . ."

[5] E.g. can. 804, § 3. Cf. *infra*. pp. 54-63.

[6] Can. 27, § 1.

[7] Cf. *supra*, p. 21.

[8] Onclin, *De Legis Indole*, p. 337; *contra*, Michiels, *Normae Generales*, I, 394, n. 1.

the general exemption accorded the traveller. It is simply a matter of present law. The Church is free to modify this general exemption and she does so in certain cases.

### 1. LAWS THAT DETERMINE THE SOLEMNITIES OF ACTS

In virtue of canon 14, §1, 2°, local statutes that determine the solemnities of acts apply to the traveller as well as to the resident. As long ago as the fourteenth century both civil and ecclesiastical jurists expressly considered the formalities of contracts in relation to local statutes. They applied the rule *locus regit actum* to contracts[9] as well as testaments and other juridic acts.[10] Since the Code of Canon Law does not incorporate the text of the rule, some authors conclude that the solemnities of public acts alone are designated by the expression *actuum solemnia.*[11] However, authors writing before the promulgation of the present law used this term in the same sense as the rule *locus regit actum.*[12] Canon 14 reaffirms the former

[9] "Aut loquimur de statuto aut de consuetudine quae respiciunt ipsius contractus solemnitatem . . . , primo casu inspicitur locus contractus . . . . "—Bartolus de Saxoferrato, *Commentaria in Primam Codicis Partem,* ad C. (1,4) 1, nn. 13-14. " . . si statutum seu consuetudo concernit solemnitatem actus adhibendam tempore contractus, tunc sive statutum sit clerici, sive laici, non valebit contractus nisi illa solemnitas fuerit observata."—Panormitanus (Nicholaus de Tudeschis), *Commentaria in Quinque Decretalium Libros* (5 vols., Venetiis, 1588), ad c. 9, X, *de foro competenti,* II, 2, n. 26.

[10] "Secundo casu quando statutum permittit id quod de iure communi etiam est permissum, sed submoveat obstaculum solemnitatis legalis, puta tot testium ut praedixi, tunc est dubium, utrum tale statutum prosit civi facienti testamentum extra territorium. Tenet ipse [Bartolus] quod non, quia quoad solemnitatem debet inspici locus ubi actus geritur nam si in aliis instrumentis consuetudo minuit solemnitatem legalem, ergo idem posse in testamentis . . ."—Petrus De Ancharano, ad c. 1, X, *de constitutionibus,* I, 2—*Repetitionum in Universas fere Iuris Canonici Partes Materiasque sane frequentiores Volumina Sex* (6 vols., Venetiis, 1583), II (*Ad primum Decretalium Librum*), 51v-52r, nn. 194, 198. Cf. also Bartolus, *Commentaria,* ad C. (1,1) 1, n. 37; Panormitanus (*Nicolaus de Tudeschis*), *Consilia Iuris, Quaestiones, et Praxis* (Venetiis, 1578), Pars II, cons. 52, nn. 1-6.

[11] Van Hove, *De Legibus Ecclesiasticis,* p. 226.

[12] " de ritualibus regula est: locus regit actum." (Ritual laws are those "quae actuum—contractuum, testamentorum, iudiciorum formam—solemnia definiunt.")—D'Annibale, *Summula Theologiae Moralis,* (5. ed., 3 vols., Romae, 1908) I, n. 204. "Insuper peregrini et vagi tenentur ad leges latas de rebus im-

law. The traveller must observe local statutes that determine the form of both public and private acts.

In determining the obligation of the traveller in this matter, civil jurists generally apply the distinction between public and private acts. The former require the intervention of a public official. Since he must act in accord with local law, the solemnities necessarily follow its prescriptions. Private acts do not require the participation of a public official. The parties are free to follow local law or the law of their homeland in respect to the solemnities that form a part of such an agreement or act.[13] Weiss teaches that the rule, even though imperative with respect to public acts, is not based upon the demands of public order.[14]

Canon 14 does not apply this distinction. The present disposition of law places a general obligation upon the traveller to conform to local statutes that secure public order or determine the solemnities of acts. This includes both public and private acts. The fact that the present law distinguishes between statutes that secure public order and those that determine the solemnities of acts does not necessarily mean that it regards the two as mutually exclusive. The rule *locus regit actum* has enjoyed a long history, and this would be a compelling motive for the legislator to include it, at least in substance, in the new law. Civil jurists are divided in the relation they recognize between the rule and laws of public order. A similar division is found among the canonists. Michiels teaches that local

mobilibus in aliquo territorio sitis et ad formas et solemnitates contractuum, iudiciorum aliorumque actuum legitimorum iure territorii in quo versatur praescriptas."—Wernz, *Ius Decretalium*, I, 130-131. "Lex localis omnes adstringit, si respiciat formam et solemnitatem contractuum, quia locus regit actum."—Marc, *Institutiones Morales Alphonsianae*, I, n. 204. Cf. also Santi, *Praelectiones Iuris Canonici*, I, tit. 2, n. 34 Ojetti, *Synopsis Rerum Moralium et Iuris Pontificii* (3. ed., 4 vols., Romae, 1909-1914), III, n. 3119, col. 2907, s.v. *peregrinus;* Noldin, *Summa Theologiae Moralis et Pastoralis* (10. ed., 3 vols., Romae, 1912), II, n. 209; Tanquerey, *Synopsis Theologiae Moralis et Pastoralis*, II, n. 290.

[13] Weiss, *Traité Théorique et Practique de Droit International Privé*, III, 118; Savigny, *Private International Law*, n. 381; Pillet, *Principes de Droit International Privé* (Paris, 1914), p. 486; *contra*, Valéry, *Manuel de Droit International Privé* (Paris, 1914), p. 538, who regarded the principle *locus regit actum* to be obligatory even with respect to private acts.

[14] *Ibid.*, pp. 102-103, cf. *supra*, pp. 34-35.

statutes determining the formalities of both public and private acts oblige the traveller in virtue of general law,[15] and that in point of fact these statutes do secure public order.[16] Sirna agrees that the solemnities of acts concern public order, and he makes no distinction between public and private juridic acts.[17]

There is some basis for this in traditional doctrine. Sanchez,[18] Laymann,[19] Ferraris,[20] and St. Alphonsus[21] made no distinction between laws that determine the forms of public and private acts. They taught that such statutes oblige the traveller, and they seemed to suggest that the reason is to be found in the same element of social necessity that always demands the traveller's obedience.

While this meaning may be read into their words, it is not at all clear. It would seem more proper to say that each statute should be judged in light of the purpose it serves. Only those that are indispensable to the protection of a necessary public good are to be regarded as laws that secure public order. Statutes that determine the formalities of public acts will generally fall into this category, but it is not certain that the same will be true with respect to private acts. They concern individuals and the protection of private rights. It is not clear that all laws determining the solemnities of private acts safeguard public order.

Thus the legislator lists as a separate classification laws that determine the solemnities of both public and private acts. Such a statute obliges the traveller primarily by reason of positive law, and secondary in the interest of public order if the statute in question is indispensable to the security of the community.

In practice the rule will rarely be applied to private acts, for the Code of Canon Law adopts local civil statutes, unless they are contrary to divine or canon law, with respect to contracts[22] and

[15] *Normae Generales, I,* 394-395.

[16] *Ibid.*, p. 394, n. 1.

[17] *De Notione Ordinis Publici in Ecclesia,* Pontificium Institutum Utriusque Iuris, Theses ad Lauream, n. 58 (Romae: apud Custodiam Librariam Pontificii Instituti Utriusque Iuris, 1949), p. 18, n. 2.

[18] *De Matrimonio,* III, disp. XVIII, n. 10.

[19] *Theologia Moralis,* I, tract. IV, cap. XII, n. 5.

[20] *Prompta Bibliotheca,* V, verbo *Lex,* art. III, n. 12.

[21] *Theologia Moralis,* I, tract. II, cap. II, dub. III.

[22] Can. 1529.

testaments.[23] In accord with the widely accepted doctrine of Private International Law, few statutes concern themselves with private juridic acts.[24]

Similarly local civil statutes that apply with the force of canon law in governing the assumption of obligations,[25] the time during which a contract obliges,[26] and the settlement of disputes by compromise,[27] oblige the traveller in virtue of general law. Their relationship to public order, however, depends upon the purpose for which each statute has been enacted.[28]

### 2. PROVISIONS AFFECTING THE SACRED LITURGY

The priest who is travelling must observe local statutes regarding the letters of identification that entitle him to be admitted to a church to celebrate Mass.[29] Some of these regulations may be intended to protect the faithful from attending the Mass of a suspended priest or to avoid some other grave and public danger. Other statutes may simply provide an orderly method of admitting a visiting priest to the church. The former statutes secure public order, while the latter do not. However, all of them oblige the traveller by reason of the general law.

At Mass the visiting priest must recite the Collect designated by the local ordinary.[30] Whenever he offers Mass in a church, public oratory, or principal semi-public oratory,[31] he must follow the local calendar.[32] While these regulations establish order in the community, it does not seem clear that they are essential to its security. Generally

[23] Cans. 1301; 1513, § 2.

[24] Cf. *supra*, p. 56; Onclin, *De Legis Indole*, p. 352.

[25] Can. 1529.

[26] Can. 33, § 2.

[27] Cans. 1926-1928.

[28] Cf. Onclin, *ibid.*, p. 338.

[29] Can. 804, § 3.

[30] S.R.C., *Dubium*, 5 martii, 1898—*Decreta Authentica Congregationis Sacrorum Rituum* (5 vols., Romae, 1898-1901; Vol. VI, 1912; Vol. VII, 1927), n. 3985 (hereafter cited as D).

[31] Therefore not in one of the minor oratories described by canon 1192, § 4.

[32] *Additiones et Variationes in Rubricis Missalis*, IV, 6; S.R.C., *Decretum*, 9 dec. 1895—D. 3862. Cardinals and bishops have the privilege of following their own calendar when travelling. Cf. cans. 239, § 1, 9°; 349, § 1, 1°.

they do not secure public order.[33] Van Hove suggests that they are applications of the principle *locus regit actum*.[34]

The Restored Order of Holy Week determines for all the Latin Rites the hours at which the liturgical functions are to take place.[35] While sufficient latitude is given to accommodate these functions to local conditions, the Holy See places special emphasis on the proper time for the Easter Vigil.[36] It is to take place at such an hour that the first Easter Mass will begin about midnight. This is in keeping with the character of the Vigil. To anticipate it by beginning the ceremony in the early evening would be out of keeping with the purpose of the solemn night watch. The Holy See does not allow the local ordinary to grant general permission to anticipate the Easter Vigil. Such exceptional permission can be given only to individual churches and localities for grave reasons of pastoral and public order.[37]

The Holy See here uses the term in a different context referring, not so much to a law, as to the reason that allows the local ordinary to depart from the rule and adapt the liturgy to a time that is suitable to local conditions. Mere convenience does not suffice to grant a permission so out of harmony with the spirit of the sacred liturgy. The Easter Vigil is the center of the Church year. It should not be deprived of its special character unless for the grave reason indicated in law. Only in the interest of public order, that is, only when anticipation of the Easter Vigil is indispensable to the safety and welfare of the community, can this permission legitimately be given.

[33] *Contra*, Michiels, *Normae Generales*, I, 395-396.

[34] *De Legibus Ecclesiasticis*, p. 227.

[35] S.R.C., decretum generale, *Liturgicus hebdomadae sanctae Ordo instauratur*, 16 nov. 1955, I, 1—*Acta Apostolicae Sedis, Commentarium Officiale* (Romae, 1909-1929; Civitate Vaticana, 1929—), XLVII (1955), 840 (hereafter cited as *AAS*).

[36] S.R.C., decretum generale, *Liturgicus hebdomadae sanctae Ordo instauratur*, 16 nov. 1955, II, 4-9—*AAS*, XLVII (1955), 840-841; *Ordinationes et declarationes circa Ordinem hebdomadae sanctae instauratum*, 1 feb. 1957, II, 4; III. 8-9; IV, 15-16; V, 19—*AAS*, XLIX (1957), 92-95.

[37] S.R.C., *Ordinationes et declarationes circa Ordinem hebdomadae sanctae instauratum*, 1 feb., 1957, V, 19, b-c—*AAS*, XLIX (1957), 94-95.

### 3. CUSTOMS REGULATING THE QUANTITY AND QUALITY OF FOOD TO BE TAKEN ON A FAST DAY

On a fast day the traveller must observe local customs[38] that determine the amount and quality of food to be taken other than at the principal meal. The law does not specify whether the place referred to is the traveller's residence or the place in which he fulfills the precept. In 1916 the Sacred Consistorial Congregation declared that the traveller is free to follow the custom of the place in which he happens to be, but apart from any obligation to do so.[39] However, in 1924 the Sacred Congregation of the Council indicated that those making the jubilee pilgrimage to Rome could obtain an indult to conform to the custom of their homeland.[40] This led most canonists to conclude that the local custom referred to in canon 1251, § 1 is the custom of the place in which the traveller fulfills the precept.[41] Onclin maintains that while the general law here requires the traveller to conform to local custom, the obligation is not based upon public order. He rightly observes that the precept to fast looks directly to the sanctification of the individual rather than to the public good.[42] Michiels agrees, but he points out that the law, while it looks to the interest of the individual, is fulfilled in a public manner. He concludes that contrary usage would easily give rise to scandal. For this reason he regards the obligation to conform to local custom as one that concerns public order.[43]

[38] In the various dioceses of the United States a uniform norm has been adopted. See "Regulations on Fast and Abstinence," adopted by the members of the American hierarchy on November 14, 1951, and reported by Bouscaren, *The Canon Law Digest* (4 vols., Vol. 1, 1917-1933; Vol. 2, 1933-1942; Vol. 3, 1942-1953; Vol. 4, 1953-1957; Milwaukee: Bruce, 1934—). III, 496-506.

[39] Sacra Congregatio Consistorialis, 31 martii 1916—*AAS*, VIII (1916), 150.

[40] Sacra Congregatio Concilii, 15 nov. 1924—Reported in Cicognani—Staffa, *Commentarium ad Librum Primum Codicis Iuris Canonici* (2 vols., Romae: ex Officina Typographica "Buona Stampa," 1939), I, 235.

[41] Van Hove, *De Legibus Ecclesiasticis*, p. 226; Michiels, *Normae Generales*, I, 396; Onclin, *De Legis Indole*, p. 338; Vermeersch—Creusen, *Epitome Iuris Canonici*, II, 401-402; Hammill, *The Obligations of the Traveller According to Canon 14*, The Catholic University of America Canon Law Studies, n. 160 (Washington, D.C.: The Catholic University of America Press, 1942), pp. 127-128.

[42] *Ibid.*, p. 338.

[43] *Ibid.*, I, 396, n. 7.

It is really not clear that contrary use would generally tend to give scandal. There might conceivably be a community in which the public conscience is so sensitive and the people so easily mislead that this could happen, but such would scarcely be the usual case. One can not assume that scandal would regularly occur as a result of failure to conform to the practice of the community.[44] Therefore, one cannot regard the obligation to follow the custom of the community as founded in the need to defend the public order.

#### 4. RESERVATION OF SINS AND CENSURES — LOCAL INTERDICT

The traveller is subject to the reservation of sins and censures effective in the place he is staying.[45] This does not mean that he is subject to the local statutes that regulate these reservations. Rather, he is indirectly affected by the fact that the confessor's jurisdiction has been restricted.

Michiels[46] suggests that the indirect effect applies to the traveller because reservations secure public order. He finds the reason for reservations expressed in canon 897. The passage cited indicates that only a few sins should be reserved. They should be grave and external. The reservation should not remain effective longer than is necessary to wipe out this public vice that has become established and to correct any harm that might have been done to ecclesiastical discipline.[47]

Reservation of cases is clearly a matter of public interest. To say that in every case it secures public order is equivalently to restrict the power of the local ordinary to those sins that present a threat to the security of the community. The reservation is a means given the local ordinary to exercise a closer and more effective control over

[44] Cf. Schmalzgrueber, *Ius Canonicum Universum*, I, pars I, tit. II, n. 42 (reported above, p. 14, n. 64)

[45] Commissio Pontificia ad Codicis Canones Authentice Interpretandos, 24 nov. 1920—*AAS*, XII (1920), 575.

[46] *Normae Generales*, I, 396-397.

[47] "Casus reservandi sunt pauci omnino, tres scilicet vel, ad summum, quatuor ex gravioribus tantum et atrocioribus criminibus externis specifice determinatis; ipsa vero reservatio ne ultra in vigore maneat, quam necesse sit ad publicum aliquod inolitum vitium extirpandum et collapsam forte christianam disciplinam instaurandam."—Can. 897.

ecclesiastical discipline. He can use this power to counteract a grave public evil, even apart from the threat it poses to society as such. Reservation is an exceptional measure, but to restrict its exercise to matters of public order would be to place greater limits on the powers of the local ordinary than the law intends. For laws that secure public order are vital to the security of the community. Whoever fails to obey them harms the society itself. Laws that secure public order do not admit of derogation in favor of individuals.

Yet the general norms for the reservation of sins provide that the restriction ceases in favor of certain sick people, for those who are preparing for marriage, whenever permission to absolve cannot be asked without grave inconvenience to the penitent or danger of violating the sacramental seal, and even in the instance that the superior refuses to grant the faculty to absolve.[48] It does not seem that a law so essential that it secures public order would admit these exceptions. It is especially difficult to understand how such a law would lose its urgent character when the very superior who supposedly recognized its urgency, upon being asked, felt that it should not be relaxed.

Furthermore, the confessor who is on a voyage by ship[49] or by air[50] has the power to absolve his fellow passengers and those who come to him for absolution. He is not restricted by reservation of sins in effect in any port of call or city through which he passes. Clearly, these exceptions would not be admitted if the reservation had the special note of urgency that is implied in laws that secure public order. The reservation extends to the traveller by reason of lack of jurisdiction on the part of the confessor.[51]

In a similar way the traveller is bound to observe a local interdict.[52] The interdict affects the place, and the general law determines

[48] Can. 900.

[49] Can. 883, § 1; Commissio Pontificia ad Codicis Canones Authentice Interpretandos, 20 maii 1923—*AAS, XVI* (1923), 114.

[50] Pius XII, motu proprio, *De facultate audiendi confessiones sacerdotibus aërium iter arripientibus concedenda,* 16 dec. 1947—*AAS XL* (1947), 17.

[51] Van Hove, *De Legibus Ecclesiasticis,* p. 227; Onclin, *De Legis Indole,* p. 339; Hammill, *The Obligations of the Traveller According to Canon 14,* pp. 121-123.

[52] Can. 2269, § 2.

that everyone present must observe it. Yet the law recognizes the possibility that one might receive a privilege not to observe it. Thus a local interdict does not necessarily secure public order. It admits of exceptions. The implication is that not every local interdict is vital to the security of the community. Otherwise, the legislator would have no right to endanger the society by granting a privilege of exemption.

## B. Local Statutes Binding the Traveler by their Own Force

Matters of public order differ according to the nature of the society concerned and, within the society itself, according to local circumstances. It would be impossible to enumerate all laws that secure public order. However, the notion will be clarified in the light of its application to certain classes of laws.

### 1. Laws that concern the organization of public offices and the exercise of public power

Laws that regulate public offices and define the rights and duties of those who exercise public power are directly concerned with the good of the community.[53] These laws are essential to the conservation of society in its present condition. They defend public order. They include statutes that govern the exercise of legislative, judicial, and administrative power, laws determining the manner of conferring ecclesiastical benefices and the administration of ecclesiastical goods.

### 2. Laws that regulate external order

Laws directed to the maintenance of good external order protect the peace and tranquillity that are essential to the community. Protection of peace is generally the care of the civil ruler, but it sometimes becomes the concern of the local ordinary. Statutes regulating

[53] Van Hove, "Leges Quae Ordini Publico Consulunt,"—*Ephemerides Theologicae Lovanienses* (Lovanii, 1924—), I (1924), 159 (hereafter cited as *ETL*); Onclin, *De Legis Indole*, pp. 339-340; Michiels, *Normae Generales*, I, 397; Le Picard, "La Notion d'Ordre Public en Droit Canonique,"—*NRT*, LV. (1928), 356; Hammill, *The Obligations of the Traveller According to Canon 14*, p. 151.

the orderly conduct of sacred processions[54] and the discipline to be observed in churches and oratories[55] secure public order.[56]

### 3. LAWS REGARDING IMMOVABLE PROPERTY

The Decretals of Gregory IX recognized the place in which immovable property is situated as a principle determining the competent forum.[57] Innocent IV (1243-1254) taught that it also means the traveller is subject to local statutes dealing with immovable property. He looked upon this as a sort of indirect subjection, for he said that the legislator's jurisdiction extends to the property. It affects the traveller only through this medium.[58] Later authors commonly regarded local statutes as extending to the traveller *ratione rei sitae*.[59] Pre-Code authors retained the doctrine.[60] The rule is reasonable, for it safeguards property rights and assures that they will be regulated in a uniform manner in each locality. Thus local statutes regarding immovable property secure public order in the ecclesiastical society. The doctrine is accepted also in the science of Private International Law.[61] Despite the long tradition behind the rule in both civil and canon law, it was not explicitly incorporated into the present law. This seems to confirm the opinion that such statutes secure public order and are implicitly included in the text of canon 14, §1, 2°.

[54] "Curent Ordinarii ut sacrae processiones, extirpatis, si qui sint, malis usibus, ordinate procedant eaque modestia ac reverentia ab omnibus perficiantur, quae piis ac religiosis huiusmodi actibus maxime convenit."—Can. 1295.

[55] Cf. cans. 1262; 1263.

[56] Onclin, *ibid.*, p. 340; Michiels, *ibid.*, p. 398; Hammill, *ibid.*, p. 152.

[57] C. 20, X, *de foro competenti*, II, 2.

[58] ". . . in rebus valet statutum, vel consuetudo, quia sunt de eius iurisdictione."—*In Quinque Libros Decretalium Commentaria* (Venetiis, 1570), ad c. 4, X, *de foro competenti*, II, 2.

[59] Bonacina, *Opera de Morali Theologia* (3 vols., Antverpiae, 1637), II, disp. 1, quaest. I, punct. VI, n. 51.

[60] ". . . [leges] reales territorio cohaerent in quo immobilia posita sunt, ideoque tenent peregrinos."—D'Annibale, *Summula Theologiae Moralis,* I, n. 204. Cf. Wernz, *Ius Decretalium,* I, n. 107, *nota* 1.

[61] "Les lois concernant la propriété appartiennent aussi au domaine des lois d'ordre public . . . . Nos anciens auteurs tenaient ces lois pour réelles quant à leur effet, c'est-à-dire territoriales, parce qu'elles sont réelles quant à leur objet. Cette raison de décider ne nous touche plus. Une loi peut avoir un immeuble

principle that the place in which a crime is committed determines the competent forum.[85] This rule governs the exercise of judicial jurisdiction. It has nothing to do with legislative power. It is a traditional rule of Roman and canon law.[86] Maroto argued that it is to be extended to legislative jurisdiction. There is some precedent for his opinion. Many early commentators interpreted the principle in a way that would suggest that it determined the scope of legislative jurisdiction as well as the competent forum.[87] They commonly taught that in virtue of this rule local penal statutes bind the traveller.[88] Suarez correctly pointed out the flaw that makes this argument unreasonable. A person cannot be guilty of a crime until first he is subject to a law.[89] It is not logical to say that the traveller is subject to local penal statutes because, if he committed a crime, he would be tried by the local tribunal. In spite of the clarity with which Suarez made his point, many authors continued to teach that, apart from ignorance of the law, the traveller is obliged to observe

gibus quae ad delicta sese referunt, quia ratione delicti fiunt subditi (c. 1566, § 1-2; 1565, § 1), ne delicta impunita maneant et ordo publicus loci facile turbetur . . . ."—Maroto, *ibid.*, I, n. 201. See also Cicognani, *Canon Law* (2. ed., authorized English version by Joseph M. O'Hara and Francis J. Brennan, Westminster, Md.: The Newman Bookshop, 1934), pp. 580-581.

[85] "Ratione delicti reus forum sortitur in loco patrati delicti."—Can. 1565, § 1.

[86] Cf. D. (48,2)22; Nov. (5)1 = Auth. post C. (3,15)2; c. 14 et 20, X, *de foro competenti*, II, 2.

[87] "A pari procedunt forum sortiri et statutis teneri."—Decius, *Super Decretalibus* (Lugduni, 1559), ad c. 7, X, *de constitutionibus*, I, 2, n. 15.

[88] "Ego credo quod iudex iudicabit secundum consuetudinem rei, cum actor forum rei sequatur, ut *Extra, de foro competenti* [II, 2], nisi ratione contractus vel maleficii factus sit de foro alterius, quia tunc servabitur consuetudo loci ubi contraxit vel ubi deliquit, ut D. VIII, *Quae contra mores* [c. 2, D. VIII] et *Extra, de foro competenti*, c. ult. [c. 20, X, *de foro competenti*, II, 2] Bar-[tholomaeus Brixiensis]"—Glossa Ordinaria, ad c. 4, D. XII s. v. *contrario more.*

[89] " . licet delictum in territorio commissum constituat hominem delinquentem talis fori . . . , tamen si ante delictum commissum non est subiectus, fieri non potest ut per delictum immediate ac simul fiat subditus."—Suarez, *De Censuris*, disp. V, sect. 5, n. 11; ". . . subiectio ad illud statutum non oritur ex delicto, sed praecise ex actuali existentia et conversatione in tali provincia."—*De Legibus*, III, c, 33, n. 8.

local penal statutes *ratione delicti.*[90] Others restricted the application to the principle to the determination of judicial competence.[91]

Maroto argued that canon 1565, §1 is to be extended to mean by reason of crime the traveller is subject to local penal statutes. He asserted that this provision is in the interest of public order, for otherwise many crimes would go unpunished.[92] The meaning of the canon is clear. It determines the competent forum, not the extent of legislative jurisdiction. The argument presented by Suarez remains sound. No one can be guilty of a crime unless he violates a law that he is bound to obey.[93] Maroto's argument, in the words of Laymann,[94] assumes what must be proved. That is to say, it must first be established that the traveller is subject to a penal law. Only then does his failure to observe it constitute a crime. Once a crime has been committed, canon 1565, §1 applies, but only to determine the competent forum. Maroto seems to have taught that, unless the forum of crime is accepted as a general principle for determining the traveller's subjection to local law, many crimes would go unpunished, and the public order would be disturbed. There is no basis for such an assumption. One cannot admit that every local

[90] " quando statutum generaliter loquitur, ita ut sit aptum comprehendere non solum subditos, sed etiam non subditos, ut si dicat: quisquis furtum fecerit in territorio meo sit excommunicatus . duo casus sunt distinguendi; nam aut forensis delinquens in territorio statuentis habet scientiam statuti aut illud ignorat. In primo casu, id est data scientia statuti, extra dubium est forensem ligari, quia forum sortitur ratione delicti."—Fagnanus, *Ius Canonicum seu Commentaria Absolutissima in Quinque Libros Decretalium* (5 vols., Romae, 1661), ad c. 21, X, *de sententia excommunicationis,* V, 39, nn. 23-24.

[91] "Si episcopus aliusve praelatus Papa inferior generalem censuram ferat, v. g. si quis talem crimen admiserit, excommunicatus est, talis censura non extendit se ad advenas et peregrinos brevi tempore ibi, non habitatione commorantes . . . . Nec satisfaciunt . . . cum aiunt, extraneos delinquentes contra statutum fieri subditos ratione delicti, ideoque censuram incurrere posse. Frustra enim assumunt quod probare debent Nos autem contra ostendimus, eas non delinquere contra statutum, quia non sunt subditi statuentis; prius enim requiritur ut aliquis sit subditus, quam ut statuto obligetur et contra illud delinquat."—Laymann, *Theologia Moralis,* I, tract. V, pars I, cap. IV, n. 5.

[92] Cf. *supra*, p. 68, n. 84.

[93] Can. 2195, § 1.

[94] Cf. *supra*, n. 91.

penal statute secures public order and imposes its obligation upon the traveller.

Michiels defends a second opinion which is based upon the distinction between vindicative and medicinal penalties. Canon 2286 indicates that vindicative penalties are directed to the expiation of crime,[95] while canon 2241, §1 states that a medicinal penalty looks to the correction of the delinquent.[96] From this distinction Michiels concludes that medicinal penalties directly seek a private good. Vindicative penalties have for their purpose the restoration of the order that has been upset by crime. Their object is to protect a public good. Thus a vindicative penalty added to a local statute serves to show that the law secures public order.[97] Medicinal penalties do not indicate that the law to which they are joined secures public order. However, the reservation of censures defends public order and protects the exercise of jurisdiction.[98]

The basis for Michiels' argument is the description of a vindicative penalty given in canon 2286. However, it seems that he draws from canons 2241, §1 and 2286 a greater distinction than they contain. These canons do not decide the long-standing dispute about the first purpose of an ecclesiastical penalty. Authors differed on this point before the promulgation of the Code of Canon Law. The dispute still goes on. The canons mentioned do not enter into the purpose of penal law in the Church. They simply indicate the formality under which vindicative and medicinal penalties are distinguished from each other. Canon 2286 is the foundation of Michiels' argument, but it does not prove, nor does it intend to prove,

[95] "Poenae vindicativae illae sunt, quae directe ad delicti expiationem tendunt ita ut earum remissio e cessatione contumaciae delinquentis non pendeat."

[96] "Censura est poena qua homo baptizatus, delinquens et contumax, quibusdam bonis spiritualibus vel spiritualibus adnexis privatur donec, a contumacia recedens, absolvatur."

[97] ". . poenae vindicativae directe ad delicti expiationem tendunt (can. 2286), seu quod idem est, ad ordinis publici tutelam; quod cum ita sit, poenae vindicativae legi adnexio per se solam abunde probat legem illam latam fuisse, quia natura sua ad 'ordini publico consulendum' est necessaria, ideoque, ad normam can. 14, § 1, 2° et ab extraneis est servandam; . . poena medicinalis seu censura, ad normam can. 2241, §1 et ss., directe et primario ad emendationem delinquentis tendit."—Michiels, *Normae Generales*, I, 401-402.

[98] *Ibid.*, I, 402, n. 1.

that vindicative penalties necessarily secure public order.[99] For this reason Michiels' opinion is to be rejected.

The simplest solution is the statement of canon 2226, §1 that whoever is bound by a law or precept is liable to the penalty it imposes unless expressly excused.[100] The traveller's liability is determined in the light of canon 14, §1, 2°. He must obey local statutes that secure public order or determine the solemnities of acts. Such a statute may contain a sanction. If the traveller disobeys the law, he is liable to the penalty; but before the element of penalty is considered, it must be established that the traveller has committed a crime. He cannot do this until he is obliged to obey the law. The penalty is not sufficient to indicate his obligation. It is an extrinsic element that does not determine the nature of the statute. A law that has for its direct and primary purpose the defense of a necessary public good is one that secures public order. Its nature is seen in the object to which the law is directed, rather than in the penalty which is added to enforce observance. Thus it cannot be established that penal laws generally, or that all vindicative penalties secure public order. Each law must be considered in the light of its purpose. The fact that it contains a sanction does not determine its relationship to public order.

### C. Responsibility of the Traveller

The traveller is not a subject of the ordinary of the place he visits. This is a norm of the general law. It is universally true, and for this reason the traveller rightly regards himself to be free, in principle, from subjection to local statutes. By way of exception, the traveller must obey local statutes that secure public order or determine the solemnities of acts.[101] This principle also is universally true, for it is a norm of general law. However, it is to be understood in consonance with the first principle that favors the traveller's freedom. When doubt arises, it is subject to strict interpretation as a restriction

[99] Roelker, "The Traveller and the Local Statute,"—*The Jurist*, II, (1942), 119.

[100] "Poenae adnexae legi aut praecepto obnoxius est qui lege aut praecepto tenetur, nisi expresse eximatur."

[101] Can. 14, § 1, 2°.

upon the traveller's liberty.[102] These two principles serve as a guide for the conduct of the traveller.

Underlying the rule is the thought that the traveller is not a part of the community. In ordinary circumstances his conduct does not affect it. In exceptional cases his actions might be harmful. They might disrupt public order. The general law provides for this by requiring the traveller to obey statutes that guard against such a danger. The law makes one further general provision for the subjection of the traveller to statutes that determine the solemnities of acts. Apart from these two cases, the traveller is free from the obligation imposed by local statutes, except in the few instances in which the general law itself makes a specific mention of his subjection.[103]

It is reasonable to expect that the traveller understands his obligation and is willing to fulfill it. He may not presume that he is free to act as he pleases. He knows that he cannot be permitted to harm the community he visits. Certain local statutes oblige him even though he is a stranger. He has the duty to discover and obey them.

The traveller is expected to take reasonable means to learn whether he is bound by a local statute. First, he should look to the text of the law. The legislator may signify his intention of extending the law to the traveller by indicating that its purpose is the defense of public order. It is not necessary that he state the reasons which prompt him to frame the law, but it is helpful if he designates as such a law that secures public order. Then the traveller's obligation is clear. The legislator's statement must be based upon fact. The situation must be such that the object of the law is to guard the public security. For it is not his intention that determines the nature of the law. This depends upon the object to which the law is ordered. Once the legislator makes this declaration, the traveller has no need to seek further. He knows that the law is directed to him. Inasmuch as the law secures public order, he has the duty to obey.

If the text of the law does not contain such a statement, the traveller must look to its purpose. This careful examination of the

[102] Can. 19.

[103] Cf. *supra*, pp. 54-63.

law is something that the resident need not do. It is sufficient that the resident knows both the meaning of the law, and that it is directed to him. Unless the law is unreasonable, and thus not a law at all, it is a true command, and he must obey. There is no question about his subjection. The case is altogether different with respect to the traveller. As a general rule he is not subject to local statutes. If the purpose of the law is not stated in the text, the traveller must examine the law to see whether he is bound. Unless his exceptional obligation is clear, the traveller rightly acts upon the presumption founded in law and regards himself as free.

In judging the purpose of a law, it is important to note that public order is not to be confused with good order and uniformity of conduct. While an orderly and well-regulated community is desirable, it is not indispensable. The superior has the power to regulate the conduct of the members of his community within reasonable limits. This power does not extend to the traveller. He is not a part of the community. He is not obliged to follow local regulations simply for the sake of uniformity. This would be an infringement upon the right to freedom of action given him in the general law. Ordinarily it is only in those matters that are indispensable to the security of the community generally that the traveller is expected to conform to local statutes.

When he examines the content of the law, the traveller will seek to learn its object. If it is a good that is essential to the security of the community, the law is one that defends public order. In some instances this will be clear. Thus a statute forbidding priests from entering a contest for public office would certainly bind the traveller. A statute requiring that priests receive the permission of the local ordinary before speaking publicly on a controversial issue is a law that secures public order.[104] In each example the statute is necessary to protect a public good that is essential to the ecclesiastical society.

In other instances the purpose of the law will not be clear. The conduct of clerics, their use of automobiles, their attendance at the theatre often are the object of local statutes. These matters do not necessarily concern public order. They can have this characteristic

[104] Roelker, "The Traveller and the Local Statute,"—*The Jurist*, II (1942), 113.

note, but it does not follow in all cases that they do. Consequently, laws that regulate these matters do not clearly secure public order.[105] When the legislator frames such a law as this, it is especially important that he should signify his purpose. If the circumstances in the community are such that the law is essential to public security, he should indicate this in the text. Then the traveller will have no doubt about his responsibility. If the legislator fails to make the purpose of the law clear, the traveller may inquire about it from the residents of the locality. Such an investigation might suggest whether circumstances exist that make the statute one of public order.

When neither the text of the law nor the matter with which it is concerned make it clear that the law secures public order, a third possibility remains. The legislator may issue an authentic interpretation of his law. By reason of his office he is qualified to declare its meaning.[106] His power to interpret law is not more extensive than his power to legislate. He cannot declare that a statute secures public order and imposes an obligation upon the traveller when the facts do not support such a claim. The public order is something objective. It exists quite apart from the superior's judgment. He legitimately declares this only when his declaration corresponds to fact. Before the legislator clarifies a doubt about the purpose of his law, the traveller rightly concludes that it does not bind him. Once an authentic interpretation has been given, the traveller has no further reason to doubt. If the superior states that a statute secures public order, the traveller must observe it. He no longer has a basis for exercising private judgment. The meaning and extent of the law are clear. The law applies to him, and he must obey.

Thus it is clear that the traveller has a duty to learn the law of the place he visits. He may not simply assume that it does not apply to him. His freedom from the jurisdiction of the local ordinary is not unlimited, and he is bound to make some effort to determine the laws that bind him. The first indication of this should appear in the text of the law itself. If this does not reveal its purpose, then it

[105] Roelker, *loc. cit.*
[106] Can. 17, § 1.

may be evident from the matter with which the law is concerned. The traveller who has examined the law from these two aspects has exercised due care. Unless the legislator has issued an authentic interpretation, the traveller must judge his obligation on the basis of what he has learned for himself. If the text of the law indicates that its purpose is to guard public order, then the traveller must consider himself bound by it. If no such statement can be found, but the matter of the law *clearly* indicates that this is its purpose, the traveller is obliged to obey. If, however, neither the text nor the matter of the law indicate *clearly* that its purpose is to secure public order, then the traveller is to regard himself as free. For the general law establishes the presumption that, apart from the exceptions indicated, he is not subject to local statutes. Unless the grounds for his subjection are clearly present, the presumption stands. He is not bound to obey.

The general law carefully protects the freedom of the traveller. It does not ordinarily impose an obligation upon him to conform to local statutes unless this is essential for the protection of the community. For his part, the traveller must have a corresponding concern lest he bring harm to the community he visits. He does this by observing those statutes that secure public order. It is worthy of mention, by way of conclusion, that these laws are established with the direct purpose of overcoming a general danger. Even if the danger is certainly absent in a particular case, the law still obliges the traveller.[107] His subjection is essential to the security of the community.

### D. Responsibility of the Local Ordinary

The local ordinary's responsibility with respect to statutes that secure public order corresponds to the traveller's obligation to obey them. The local ordinary exercises care over a certain territory. His jurisdiction enables him to provide for its needs. He can make suitable laws, exercise judgment, and enact penalties to this end. He must exercise this power within the norms established by general law.[108] He has no right to go beyond these limits. To do so would be to act unlawfully. It would be a misuse of authority.

[107] Can. 21.

[108] Can. 335, § 1.

His legislative power is directed to the welfare of the community and its members. His subjects are determined by their domicile or quasi-domicile and actual presence. Normally these people are the only ones obliged to observe his laws.[109] In doing so, they contribute to the common good of the community to which they belong.

The traveller is not his subject. He is not a member of the community, and as a rule, he is not bound to obey its laws. Nevertheless, he may not harm the community he visits.[110] He must obey those laws that are necessary to preserve its security. They have for their object something more than the common good. Their object falls under the general heading of public good, but it is more specific. It is a public good that is essential to the society as such. The formal aspect under which public order differs from public good is that the former is absolutely essential to the security of the community. Reason demands that a law of such importance should oblige everyone. For whoever disobeys it, whether he be a subject or not, inflicts the same harm upon the community. Accordingly, the general law determines that the traveller is subject to local statutes that secure public order. By way of exception, it confers corresponding jurisdiction upon the local ordinary. Apart from such exceptional jurisdiction given him in this and in a few other instances, the local ordinary has no authority over the traveller. This is a very important principle. It is the norm of general law. It establishes the presumption that the traveller is free from all subjection to local statutes, except where the general law itself provides otherwise.

Consequently, the notion of public order is one of great importance to the local ordinary. His office requires that he preserve this order. for the safety of the community depends upon it. Yet he may not use this duty as a pretext for legislating beyond the limits of his jurisdiction.

The relationship between public order and certain local statutes is immediately clear. It is apparent that their object is to protect a good that is essential to the security of the community. Laws that concern the organization of the society and the distribution and exercise of public power, laws made to remove a cause of constant

[109] Can. 13, § 2.

[110] Vermeersch—Creusen, *Epitome Iuris Canonici,* I, 111-112.

and grave scandal to the community, clearly secure public order. On the other hand, there are laws that have a relationship with public order that is not so apparent. They might be directed to the removal of a danger that, while it is grave, public, and social in character, is a consequence of conditions proper to this community. The traveller, being a stranger, is not expected to know of such local conditions. It will not be clear to him at first that such a law defends public order. He may discover this upon investigation, and it is reasonable to expect that he will make some effort to learn whether a local statute applies to him. However, his doubts will quickly be resolved if the local ordinary specifies the purpose of his law.

The first way in which the local ordinary may designate the purpose of the law is by stating it in the text. Phrases like *"ad tuendam securitatem,"* or *"ad tuendum ordinem"* suffice.[111] They indicate the purpose of the law without going into needless detail about the underlying reasons. It would be advantageous if the legislator used such a phrase to identify every statute that secures public order. This is especially helpful, and in some cases even necessary, if the purpose of the law is not immediately clear. It is true that the traveller is expected to make some effort to discover for himself the purpose of the law. Failing to find a clear indication that it secures public order, he rightly acts upon the presumption favoring freedom unless the legislator has himself declared its purpose.

The second way the legislator can designate the purpose of his law is by an authentic interpretation of an already existing statute. He is competent to explain the meaning and scope of his own laws,[112] but his power to interpret is no greater than his power to make laws. Whether in framing the law or in giving an authentic interpretation, his declaration must correspond to fact, or it means nothing. Public order is something objective. When the legislator declares that a statute secures public order, he merely states what is already true. The purpose of the law may not be clear. His statement may be necessary to make it known, but it has no significance unless grounded in fact.

[111] Roelker, *art. cit.*, p. 110.
[112] Can. 17, § 1.

It follows that the legislator has a serious duty in this regard to exercise prudent judgment. When he legislates for the traveller, it must be from the reasoned conviction that this is essential to the security of the community. The legislator who would attempt to bind the traveller to his laws for reasons of uniformity or for some other motive not admitted in the general law would exceed the limits of his jurisdiction. If he declared a law to be for the defence of public order and the facts did not substantiate his statement, his action would be a misuse of authority. It would be an unjustified attempt to deprive the traveller of the freedom accorded him in the Code of Canon Law. Such an act would constitute a serious abuse of office. Therefore, the legislator must exercise a two-fold responsibility. He must protect the community by appropriate legislation, and he must respect the traveller's right to freedom.

## Article II. Public Order and the Community of Life in Marriage

Laws of public order may be found in many fields. Le Picard applies the notion to the common life of husband and wife.[113] This is customarily described as cohabitation and sharing of bed and board. Le Picard analyzes the three aspects of married life inasmuch as they depend upon natural and divine positive law, ecclesiastical and civil law, and the principles of sociology. He explains the nature of the obligation as well as the power required to modify it and authorize a complete or partial separation.

When a man and woman marry, they form a society and, by mutual agreement, enter upon a common life. The nature of marital life is already established, quite apart from the will of those who enter upon it.[114] The principal obligation is to share the same home.[115] The sharing of bed and board is traditionally[116] joined with

[113] *La Communauté de la Vie Conjugale, Obligation des Époux* (Paris: Librairie du Recueil Sirey, 1930).

[114] *Ibid.*, pp. 1-2.

[115] "Nous ne prétendons certes pas la faire passer avant le grand devoir des époux, celui qui résume si bien leur engagement réciproque, qu'on a pu l'appeller le devoir conjugal; ce devoir-là appartient à la 'substance' même du mariage. Nous disons simplement qu'elle est le principal élément de la communauté de vie qui s'ajoute au mariage pour en faire 'l'integrité'."—*Ibid.*, p. 16.

[116] "Verum, quia in huiusmodi dubietate fama viciniae magis debet attendi,

cohabitation to form the three-fold obligation of common life in marriage. Each aspect has a different foundation that determines its proper force.

Cohabitation is a natural accompaniment of marriage. It is by sharing the same home that husband and wife are able to have and to educate their children and to give to each other the aid and support that is proper to their state in life. Refusal to live together would disrupt the order established by God and stand as an obstacle to the fulfillment of the purposes of marriage. This conduct would affect the community as well as the parties, for it would render impossible the proper education of children. Therefore, the obligation of cohabitation is much more than a private matter. Inasmuch as the obligation affects the security of the society, it concerns the public order.[117]

The sharing of bed and board are of no direct interest to the society as such. If these obligations involve the public good in a particular instance, the relationship is accidental. Husband and wife enjoy greater freedom in this regard than they do with respect to the duty to dwell together.[118]

Le Picard goes on to discuss the competence of Church and state with regard to the marital obligations of life in common. Certain reasons will allow husband and wife to modify their mode of life with respect to bed and board, even apart from the intervention of public authority.[119] Both these obligations are private in nature.

*tuae sollicitudinis erit fama loci diligenter inquirere, utrum praedictus vir eam in lecto et in mensa sicut suam uxorem aut concubinam habuerit;* et si fama loci habet, quod vir ipsam in lecto et in mensa sicut uxorem tenuerit, quum matrimonium sit maris et feminae coniunctio, individuam vitae consuetudinem retinens: cogenda est mulier, ut eidem viro affectu serviat coniugali "—c. 11, X, *de praesumptionibus,* I, 23.

[117] *Ibid.*, pp. 64-65.

[118] "A la différence de la cohabitation, la communauté de lit et de table n'intéresse pas directement la société. Il n'est pas impossible que le bien public soit en cause; mais ce ne sera que d'une manière accidentelle, de sorte qu'à cet égard les époux ont ordinairement une liberté dont ils ne jouissent pas en ce qui concerne l'obligation de vivre dans la même maison."—*Ibid.*, pp. 67-68.

[119] *Ibid.*, pp. 68, 72.

They do not directly affect the public good.[120] When special circumstances cause this conduct to affect the society, the Church has the right to intervene to protect the public good. However, their obligation to share the same home always has a direct and vital effect upon society. It is a matter of public order, for the law itself indicates the extent of the obligation and the causes that justify separation.[121] Very often the intervention of the public authority is necessary in order to give juridic effect to their separation, and this properly falls within the competence of the Church.

Le Picard's study is of special interest, for it serves to illustrate that the notion of public order is involved in problems other than that of the traveller and the local statute. At the same time this study gives the opportunity to observe the practical application of the norm he suggests for distinguishing public order and public good. He regards public order as something stable and unchanging, as determined and protected by law. Public order is disturbed only when the law that secures it is violated. A peril to the community that arises from circumstances not foreseen in the law involves the public good, but it does not concern public order.

In the matter at hand the obligation of cohabitation is spelled out in law, for it directly and regularly concerns the welfare of society. The sharing of bed and board are private matters. They entail a juridic obligation, but its interest is generally limited to the spouses. When special circumstances arise to make the obligation one of interest to the community, it begins to involve the public good. Partial separation of husband and wife then require the intervention of public authority. The reason is not to be found

[120] " . . la communauté de lit quotidienne ou habituelle, qui a pour suite naturelle les relations conjugales, constitue certes un droit pour la partie, et qui peut être revendiqué devant un tribunal ecclésiastique, mais que le bien public n'y est pas directement intéressé Le bien public ne sera pas davantage compromis si la communauté de table n'est pas observée . Elle risque fort d'apparaître comme le témoignage d'un désaccord. Toutefois, par lui-même, ce désaccord n'est pas tellement grave et surtout n'offre pas en général un tel charactère de publicité que la société s'en trouve lésée et doive s'en préoccuper."—*Ibid.*, p. 82.

[121] *Ibid.*, pp. 44-66.

in the need to secure public order, but in the need to protect the public good.[122]

## Article III. Public Order and Canonical Sanctions

Canonists disagree about the fundamental purpose of ecclesiastical penalties. In view of the several opinions proposed, one cannot state with certainty that the natural object of every penalty is the protection or the restoration of public order.[123] It is a general principle of canon law that interpretation of penalties in doubtful matters should be favorable to the subject.[124] Since it cannot be established that all penalties secure public order, or that all vindicative penalties do, one must conclude that local statutes do not, solely by reason of the penalty annexed to them, impose an obligation on the traveller.[125] While the reflex principle solves a practical problem, it does not reach the heart of the matter. The question of the relationship between public order and penalties in general, or vindicative penalties in particular, remains unanswered.

In the field of Private International Law penal statutes are regarded as imposing an absolute obligation upon nationals and aliens alike. Jurists of the Italian and French school explain that penal laws as a class are laws of public order.[126] There is a great

[122] *Ibid.*, pp. 82-85. For an evaluation of Le Picard's criterion for distinguishing public order and public good, see above, pp. 45-48.

[123] Cf. *supra*, pp. 68-72. Thus while Wernz—Vidal teach that the purpose of a canonical penalty is the need to restore public order, they do not regard the traveller generally to be subject to sanctions established by local statutes. Cf. *Ius Canonicum ad Codicis Normam Exactum* (7 vols. in 8, Romae: apud Aedes Universitatis Gregorianae, 1923-1948), Vol. I (2. ed., 1951), 204; Vol. VII (2. ed., 1951), 180-184 (hereafter cited as *Ius Canonicum*).

[124] Can. 2291, § 1.

[125] Van Hove, *De Legibus Ecclesiasticis*, p. 224; Onclin, *De Legis Indole*, p. 351; *contra*, Michiels, *Normae Generales*, I, 400-401.

[126] "L'étranger qui se sera rendu coupable en France d'un délit, et nous pensons ici le mot délit dans son acceptation la plus étendue, sera donc puni et puni comme un Français le serait lui-même à sa place, non pas comme on l'a dit, parce qu'il est devenu le sujet du pays où il s'est transporté, mais parce que la necessité le veut aussi, l'État ne pouvant assurer l'ordre qu'à la condition de confondre au point de vue de la répression, les étrangers et les nationaux."—Pillet, *De l'Ordre Public en Droit International Privé*, p. 19; "Les lois penales et les lois de police et de sûreté publique sont obligatoire pour tous ceux qui se

difference of opinion as to the foundation for penalties in civil law.[127] Italian and French jurists writing at the time of promulgation of the Code of Canon Law widely accepted the juridic theory. This theory has been outlined by Latini (1857-1938) in a book that has exerted considerable influence on recent canonical doctrine.[128] Latini distinguishes three orders in society. There is the moral order, which exists when men freely act in accord with the eternal law of order. When they act contrary to this law, moral disorder follows as a result.[129]

In man's present condition it is the function of civil society to guarantee the possession and exercise of his rights and the fulfillment of his obligations. Society affords this protection to the individual so that he may be able to achieve his end. It guarantees a state of juridic order. When the individual's rights go unprotected and he is hindered from gaining his end, society is in a state of juridic disorder.[130]

In any civil society the individual, who otherwise would not be secure in the possession of his rights, enjoys the protection of law and the resulting confidence that are essential if he is to live in peace and safety. This is the state of public order. If flows from the nature of society and is the logical and inviolable consequence of juridic order. Security under law and the confidence this engenders are the social rights of every individual. Public order is social or political order, for it is realized under the protection of the city or the state.[131]

The penal power of the state is derived from the notion of public order. The right to punish arises from the need to restore this order after an individual harms it through the abuse of his liberty. The cause of punitive power is the disruption of public

trouvent sur le territoire du royaume."—Art. 11, Italian Civil Code of 1865, reported by Mancini, *JDIP,* I (1874), 300.

[127] Cf. Latini, *Iuris Criminalis Philosophici Summa Lineamenta* (Taurini—Romae: Marietti, 1924), 1-44.

[128] *Ibid.*, pp. 37-44.

[129] *Ibid.*, p. 37.

[130] *Ibid.*, p. 38.

[131] *Ibid.*, pp. 38-39.

order. Its purpose is the restoration of order and peace. Its measure is in proportion to the harm that has been visited upon society.[132]

In accord with the juridic theory every penalty, by its very nature, secures public order. As a logical consequence all penal laws must be regarded as laws that are absolutely imperative and bind the alien to the same extent that they oblige the citizen. Civil jurists commonly follow this in practice by regarding penal statutes as laws of public order.[133]

Canonists are not agreed that the same principle holds true in church law. The fundamental purpose of ecclesiastical penalties is sharply disputed. For convenience the various opinions can be divided into three groups. Some hold that punitive power has the same basis in the Church as in civil society. That is to say, the canonical penalty has for its principal purpose the restoration of public order.[134]

Vidal (1867-1938) turns to Latini's explanation of the nature of public order and its relationship to punitive power.[135] The need to restore public order is the basis for the power to punish. The threat of punishment secures public order, while the infliction of a penalty establishes again the order that has been disturbed by crime.[136] In the Church the supreme and essential purpose of every sanction is

[132] *Ibid.*, p. 43.

[133] Cf. *supra*, p. 82, n. 126.

[134] Wernz, *Ius Decretalium*, I, n. 73; Ottaviani, *Compendium Iuris Publici Ecclesiastici* (4. ed., Romae: Typis Polyglottis Vaticanis, 1954), pp. 185-188; Roberti, *De Delictis et Poenis* (2. ed., Romae: apud Custodiam Librariam Pontificii Instituti Utriusque Iuris, 1944), I, 247-251.

[135] Wernz—Vidal, *Ius Canonicum*, VII, 24-28.

[136] "Ex dictis apparet formulam, qua debet enuntiari principium de origine iuridica poenae seu potestatis puniendi, esse hanc, necessitatem conservationis seu tutelae publici ordinis socialis. Inde quidem habet poena, quod in statu comminationis deterreat a legis violatione, et in hoc sensu est sanctio legis, legem ipsam firmat et ordinem iuridicum contra perturbatores tuetur et protegit: in statu executionis restaurat ordinem socialem laesum, est reactio ordinis contra deordinationem . . . . Inde etiam patet finem intrinsicum poenae esse restitutionem ideoque conservationem et tuitionem publici ordinis in societate: implicite tamquam sequelae obtinetur ut plurimum, correctio delinquentis, pravorum intimidatio, securitas in bonis, et consequens securitas et tranquillitas publica, finis ultimus auctoritatis publicae ut talis."—*Ibid.*, pp., 27-28.

the restoration and protection of the ecclesiastical public order.[137] This is the object to which every penalty is directed.[138] The penalty has additional extrinsic purposes which it may also serve. It may prevent the criminal act, cause the criminal to repent his misdeed, or serve as a salutary example to others.[139] Not all these purposes will be served in each instance. Besides its primary object a penalty may be directed to one or more of these. However, to say that a penalty is directed only to the correction of the individual and not the restoration of public order is to confuse its nature and extrinsic purpose.[140] The first purpose of all penalties is the same. It is the restoration of public order.

The second opinion, proposed by Michiels,[141] is based upon the important distinction between the ecclesiastical and the civil societies. By divine institution the Church is directed towards a supernatural end. Its purpose is the salvation of souls. The Church is concerned directly and immediately with an external and public good, the sanctification of all its members, not as individuals, but as members of the ecclesiastical society.[142] Quite unlike other perfect societies,

137 " . . finis poenarum ecclesiasticarum *ultimus* et *supremus* atque vere *essentialis* est *conservatio* et *tutela* ordinis socialis in Ecclesia per delictum violati et *per poenam restaurandi*."—*Ibid.*, pp. 180-181.

138 ". . . potestas punitiva, quae complementum est potestatis legiferae efficacis, dum poenam socialem delicti infligit, directe intendit restaurare ordinem moralem publicum delicto laesum, ad quem, tamquam medium ad finem, malum poenae inflictae ordinatur."—*Ibid.*, p. 182.

139 *Ibid.*, p. 183.

140 *Ibid.*, pp. 183-184, *contra*, Lega, *Praelectiones in Textum Iuris Canonici de Iudiciis Ecclesiasticis* (4 vols., Romae, 1896-1901), III, 8-9 (hereafter cited as *De Iudiciis Ecclesiasticis*).

141 *De Delictis et Poenis* (Lublin: Universitas Catholica, 1934—), I, 18-21; *Normae Generales*, I, 400-402. See also Cicognani—Staffa, *Commentarium ad Librum Primum Codicis Iuris Canonici*, I, 228-229; Rodrigo, *Praelectiones Theologico-Morales Comillenses*, Series I, *Theologia Moralis Fundamentalis*, Tomus II, *Tractatus de Legibus* (Santander: Sal Terrae, 1944), 142.

142 "*Ut quaevis societate perfecta*, i.e. ex natura sua generica, Ecclesia directe et immediate respicit bonum spirituale *externum* et *publicum*, ipsi societati ecclesiasticae qua tali commune, quatenus scilicet non uniuscuiusque membri, qua singuli, sanctificationem prosequitur, sed sanctificationem omnium membrorum, prout pars sunt societatis ecclesiasticae externae . . . ."—Michiels, *De Delictis et Poenis*, I, 20.

however, the Church has for her principal care the spiritual good of the individual.[143]

The Church fulfills this two-fold purpose in the exercise of her power to teach and to sanctify as well as to rule, that is, to legislate, to judge, and to punish. When these social powers are used for the sanctification of the individual, the Church exercises jurisdiction in the internal forum. It is a vicarious power used with regard to the relationship between man and God. When this power is used for the public good of the society, it is jurisdiction in the external forum. This is a proper power, for it pertains to the society as such.[144]

The foundation of punitive power in the Church as well as in the state is the protection of the external and public good. However, there is a fundamental difference which must be taken into consideration. The protection of social juridic order is an end in itself for civil society, while in the Church it is a means to achieve the final end to which the society is directed, the sanctification of the individual.[145] Thus when the Church imposes a penalty in the external forum, its first purpose is the restoration of public order; but the sanction must also serve to bring about the correction of the individual if this is possible.[146] It is in this sense that a canonical penalty is defined as the deprivation of some good, inflicted by

[143] "At insuper, imo praecipue, *ut societas perfecta spiritualis prorsus peculiaris,* seu ex indole specifica ad bonum aeternum procurandum ordinata, Ecclesia directe et immediate promovere debet *singulorum* membrorum sanctificationem . . . ." —*Loc. cit.*

[144] *Loc. cit.*

[145] "Et revera, ad momentum quod attinet, dum in societate civili tutela ordinis juridici socialis est finis in se, et quidem adequatus, ita ut praeter illam nullus alius finis ab auctoritate civili directe sit prosequendus ideoque in poenis inferendis directe et principaliter nullatenus intendatur singulorum civium bonum et emendatio delinquentium, in Ecclesia, e contra, tutela ordinis juridici socialis non est finis in se, sed solummodo medium, ex intentione Fundatoris ad finem supernaturalem ultimum, id est sanctificationem singulorum, positive dirigendum." —*Ibid.,* p 21.

[146] "Inde sequitur quod Ecclesia, cum in foro externo poenas irrogat, praeprimis sane et magis directe de ordine publico restaurando curat, ita ut in suo systemate poenali ab indole retributionis socialis poenarum abstrahere non valeat, sed insuper curat, imo curare debet, ut vindicta socialis, quae est poenae intrinsice propria, pro posse insimul in sanctificationem, idest in emendationem singulorum delinquentium concurrat."—*Ibid.,* pp. 21-22.

legitimate authority, to bring about the correction of the individual and the punishment of crime.[147] In this same sense the Church distinguishes between vindicative and medicinal penalties. The former are directed more to the punishment of crime and the restoration of public order, while the latter are more in the interest of the individual's salvation.[148] Therefore, vindicative penalties secure public order by their very nature; medicinal penalties do not.[149]

The third opinion concerning the nature of penalties is based upon the assertion that Church and state exercise their powers in an entirely different manner.[150] Civil authority is directed to temporal welfare, and it uses penalties to counteract crimes that disturb peace and temporal order. The Church, by reason of her mission, punishes those acts that disturb the supernatural order. The state punishes crime because it harms society. The Church looks rather to the criminal than to the crime and seeks to bring about his correction. Penalties have for their first purpose to move the criminal to penance and to remove the danger of scandal. Canonical penalties are applied, not so much because crime disturbs the social order, as by reason of the danger it presents to the welfare of souls.[151] They are directed to the spiritual good of the individual. This is true of all ecclesiastical penalties, for it follows from the nature of the Church and the exercise of her power. It is true even of penalties that are directed specifically to the public good. Penalties are always related to the spiritual welfare of the individual, for the purpose of the Church and also of every canonical institute is the salvation of souls.

[147] Can. 2215.

[148] Cans. 2241; 2286.

[149] *Ibid.*, p. 22.

[150] Hollweck, *Die kirchlichen Strafgesetze* (Mainz, 1899), p. 84; Lega, *De Iudiciis Ecclesiasticis,* III, 8-9.

[151] "Ex supra allatis animadversionibus sponte sua fluit diversitas quae intercedit maxima et essentialis inter systema poenale Ecclesiae et Reipublicae civilis. —Haec enim crimina persequitur quatenus sunt malum in societate, et, ea puniendo, vindicat iura eiusdem societatis; Ecclesia in criminosis potiusquam in crimina animadvertit, maxime ut eos ad poenitentiam adducat, scandalum auferat et animarum perniciem, atque in criminibus detestatur directius et principalius non infractiones legis seu ordinis socialis, sed iacturam sanctificationis animarum."—Lega, *ibid.*, p. 8.

These three are the principal opinions about the foundation of punitive power in the Church. The question was disputed before promulgation of the Code of Canon Law, and the legislator did not offer a solution. A detailed study of this question is beyond our purpose, but a few observations are indicated.

It seems evident that public order is subject to a very specific interpretation in canon law. It is conformity to a law that is indispensable to the security of the Church as a society. Laws that secure public order have for their object a necessary public good. To say that by their nature penalties conserve public order would be to restrict the punitive power of the Church to those instances in which it is indispensable to her security. This does not seem to be in accord with the mission of the Church to use all her powers for the salvation of souls. For it would deprive the Church of the right to inflict a penalty in order to bring about the sanctification of the individual. Granting this were true, the local ordinary would be incapable of establishing a penalty to enforce a law that was intended to foster greater holiness or learning among his priests, or that was intended to create greater esteem for the clerical state. It seems rather that in determining the foundation of ecclesiastical penalties one must take into account the unique nature of the Church and her mission to teach, govern, sanctify, and save all men. It is not possible to apply the civil concept of punitive power to the ecclesiastical society without taking into consideration that the Church must concern herself with the eternal salvation of each one of her members. This is the ultimate object of her laws and the purpose to which she directs the exercise of all her powers.

It does not seem that the nature of canonical sanctions is to be found in the distinction between vindicative and medicinal penalties. The distinction was recognized before the promulgation of the Code of Canon Law. The dispute existed then, and it still exists. Canons 2241 and 2286 do not solve it. Indeed, these canons only indicate the formality under which vindicative and medicinal penalties are to be distinguished from each other. They do not intend to define the nature of a penalty as such. The argument deduced from these canons, namely, that vindicative penalties secure public order while medicinal penalties do not, must be rejected.

The answer to the problem seems to lie in the intimate nature of the Church and the purpose to which she directs the exercise of her powers. The Church is a supernatural society. Her purpose is the salvation of souls. Every canonical institute is directed to this end.[152] It would be a limitation placed upon her functions to restrict the exercise of punitive power to those matters concerning the society as such. Her laws are directed to the sanctification of the individual, and it would seem reasonable to expect that canonical penalties have the same object. They are not restricted to matters of public order. These concern the security of the ecclesiastical society. Church law embraces these matters within its scope, but it extends beyond to include the sanctification of the individual as well. It would seem that punitive power has the same broad extension.

Onclin[153] points out that medieval canonists more commonly regarded penalties as directed to the correction of the individual and as an example to the faithful than a means to bring about the restoration of a disturbed social order.[154] Many of them taught that the traveller is subject to local penal statutes by reason of the principle that determines the judicial forum *ratione delicti.*[155] Suarez rightly observed that the rule governs judicial and not legislative jurisdiction.[156] However, some of them reasoned that the obligation arose from the very nature of a penalty. They regarded penalties to be medicinal because directed to the salvation of souls,

[152] "Quicumque ergo ecclesiasticus doctor ecclesiasticas regulas ita interpretatur aut moderatur, ut ad regnum charitatis cuncta quae docuerit vel exposuerit, referat, nec peccat, nec errat: cum saluti proximorum consulens, ad finem sacris institutionibus debitum pervenire intendat."—Ivo Carnutensis, *Prologus*—*MPL,* 161, 47-48.

[153] *De Legis Indole,* p. 348.

[154] "Est tamen generalius intelligendum quo ad correctionem hominum pertinet, nam sive plectendo, sive ignoscendo hoc solum bene agitur, ut vita hominum corrigatur. 23 q. 5, *prodest* [c. 4, C. XXIII, q. 5]."—Hostiensis (Henricus de Segusio), *Summa Aurea* (Venetiis, 1570), lib. V, tit. *de poenis,* 37, n. 5. The passage to which he refers in *Decretum Gratiani* is taken from a letter of St. Augustine to Macedonius—Epistola 153, n. 19—*MPL,* 33, 662. "Poenae sunt medicinae . . . "—Boich, *In Quinque Decretalium Libros Commentaia* (Venetiis, 1576), ad c. 1, X, *de poenis,* V, 37, n. 3.

[155] Cf. *supra,* p. 69, n. 87.

[156] Cf. *supra,* p. 69, n. 89.

and consequently to be favors applicable to the traveller as well as the subject.[157] Later, Fagnanus taught the same doctrine.[158]

Canonists and theologians from the sixteenth century contributed much to the development of a theory determining the traveller's subjection to local statutes. Many did not expressly declare that penal statutes have the element of social necessity that requires obedience from the traveller.[159] Others clearly stated that penal statutes do not ordinarily bind the traveller.[160] Some of those who taught that the traveller is subject to local penalties argued from the principle that determines judicial competence *ratione delicti.* The principle has no relation to legislative jurisdiction. For this reason their doctrine is to be rejected.

There is no constant canonical tradition declaring penalties by nature to be directed to the conservation of public order. The distinction between vindicative and medicinal penalties does not afford an indication of the fundamental purpose of punitive power. There is no sound reason to reject the teaching, already solidly grounded in canonical tradition, that penalties, like all other institutes of church law, are directed to the salvation of souls. Penalties add sanctions to already existing legal obligations. They do not change the purpose of laws. Penalties do not necessarily secure public order. They have this effect only when they are joined to laws that are

[157] "Videtur tamen quod non subditi nullo modo astringantur. Si enim episcopus facit indulgentiam, non participant ei non subditi . . . . Sed si non participant in gratia, quae favorabilis est . . multo minus in poena, quae est odiosa . . . . Solutio: Haec eadem ratio diversum pactum reformat: utrumque enim diversum verum est, scilicet quod indulgentiae non participat non subditus, ut in contrario, et quod sententiam excommunicationis incurrit, ut hic. Et est ratio eadem utriusque: salus scilicet animarum; ideo enim indulgentiae non participat, ne poenitentiae enerventur, quod et expedit animabus . . . ideo etiam hanc sententiam incurrit ut medicina percepta de delicto quod commisit citius poenitentiam agat, quod et sentire expedit animabus."—Hostiensis (Henricus de Segusio), *In Quinque Decretalium Gregorianarum Libros Commentaria* (Venetiis, 1581), ad. c. 21, X, *de sententia excommunicationis,* V, 39, n. 3.

[158] *Ius Canonicum seu Commentaria Absolutissima in Quinque Libros Decretalium* (5 vols., Romae, 1661), IV, ad c. 21, X, *de sentientia excommunicationis,* V, 39, n. 25.

[159] Cf. *supra,* pp. 7-15.

[160] Cf. *supra,* p. 70, n. 91.

indispensable to the security of the ecclesiastical society as such, that is, to laws that have for their direct object the protection of a necessary public good.

## CONCLUSIONS

1. The term *public order* was in use among canonists as early as the last quarter of the nineteenth century. It is certain that the Code of Canon Law did not introduce the term into canonical literature. [Cf. p. 21-25.]

2. The several canonists who introduced the term into canonical jurisprudence used it to express the commonly accepted doctrine regarding the traveller's subjection to local statutes. [Cf. pp. 21-25.]

3. The norm for interpretation of public order in the Church is the law defining the traveller's subjection to local statutes as it was commonly acknowledged before the promulgation of the Code of Canon Law. [Cf. pp. 39-41.]

4. Public order may be defined as a pattern of conduct in conformity with a law that is essential to the security of the society in that it is indispensable to the protection of a necessary public good. [Cf. pp. 41-49.]

5. The term has a general application and is not restricted to the frame of reference of the traveller and the local statute. [Cf. pp. 59, 79-91.]

6. The obligation of cohabitation, one aspect of the community life in marriage, is essential to the security of society. It is a matter of public order. [Cf. pp. 79-82.]

7. Canonical penalties do not necessarily secure public order. They have this effect only when they are joined to laws that are indispensable to the security of the ecclesiastical society as such, that is, to laws that have for their direct object the protection of necessary public good. [Cf. pp. 82-91.]

# BIBLIOGRAPHY

## Sources

*Acta Apostolicae Sedis, Commentarium Officiale,* Romae, 1909-1929; Civitate Vaticana, 1929—

Bouscaren, T. Lincoln, *The Canon Law Digest,* 4 vols., Vol. 1, 1917-1933; Vol. 2, 1933-1942; Vol. 3, 1942-1953; Vol. 4, 1953-1957; Milwaukee: The Bruce Publishing Co.

*Codex Iuris Canonici Pii X Pontificis iussu digesta, Benedicti Papae XV auctoritate promulgatus, Praefatione, Fontium Annotatione et Indice Analytico-Alphabetico ab Emo Petro Card. Gasparri Auctus,* Romae: Typis Polyglottis Vaticanis, 1917; reimpressio, 1934.

*Corpus Iuris Canonici,* editio Lipsiensis II, post Aemilii Ludovici Richteri curas instruxit Aemilius Friedberg, Lipsiae: Ex officina Berhardi Tauchnitz, 1879-1881; ed. anastatice repetita, 1928.

*Corpus Iuris Civilis,* 3 vols., Berolini, 1928-1929; *Institutiones,* quas recognovit P. Krueger; *Digesta,* quae recognovit T. Mommsen et retractavit P. Krueger; *Codex Instinianus,* quem recognovit et retractavit P. Krueger.

*Corpus Iuris Civilis,* Lugduni, 1553-1557.

*Decreta Authentica Congregationis Sacrorum Rituum,* 5 vols., Romae, 1898-1901, Vol. VI, 1912; Vol. VII, 1927.

*Decretales D. Gregorii Papae IX, suae integritati una cum glossis restitutae, cum privilegio Gregorii XIII, Pont. Max., et aliorum Principum,* Romae, 1582.

*Decretum Gratiani emendatum et notionibus illustratum cum glossis, Gregorii XIII, Pont. Max. iussu editum,* 2 vols., Romae, 1582.

*Liber Sextus Decretalium D. Bonifacii Papae VIII, suae integritati cum Clementinis et Extravagantibus, earumque glossis restitutus,* Romae, 1582.

*Missale Romanum, seu ex decreto Sacrosancti Concilii Tridentini restitutum, S. Pii V, Pontificis Maximi iussu editum, aliorum cura recognitum, a Pio X reformatum et Benedicti XV auctoritate vulgatum.*

## Reference Works

Aquino, S. Thomas de, *Commentarium in Decem Libros Ethicorum,* Parisiis, 1875.

———, *Commentarium in De Divinis Nominibus,* Parisiis, 1889.

———, *Summa Theologiae,* Pars Prima et Prima Secundae, cura et studio Sac. Petri Caramello, Taurini—Romae: Marietti, 1950.

Azpilcueta, Martinus (Navarrus). *Enchiridion sive Manuale Confessariorum et Poenitentium,* Wirceburgi, 1593.

Bargilliat, Michael, *Praelectiones Iuris Canonici,* 10. ed., Parisiis, 1899.

Bartolus de Saxoferrato, *Opera Omnia,* 11 vols., Venetiis, 1590-1595.

Boich, Henricus, *In Quinque Decretalium Libros Commentaria,* Venetiis, 1576.

Bonacina, Martinus, *Opera de Morali Theologia,* 3 vols., Antverpiae, 1637.

Brys, Iosephus, *Tractatus de Legibus,* Brugis: apud Editiones Car. Beyaert, 1942.

Cappello, Felix, *Summa Iuris Canonici*, 4. ed., 3 vols., Romae: apud Aedes Universitatis Gregorianae, 1945-1955.

Cicognani, Amleto G., *Canon Law*, 2. ed., authorized English version by Joseph M. O'Hara and Francis J. Brennan, Westminster, Md.: The Newman Bookshop, 1934.

——— —Staffa, Dinus, *Commentarium ad Librum Primum Codicis Iuris Canonici*, 2 vols., Romae: ex Officina Typographica "Buona Stampa," 1939.

Cocchi, Guidus, *Commentarium in Codicem iuris canonici ad usum scholarum*, 4. ed., 8 vols., Taurinorum Augustae: Marietti, 1931-1946.

Covarruvias y Leyva, Didacus, *Opera Omnia*, 2 vols., Coloniae, 1579.

D'Annibale, Iosephus, *Summula Theologiae Moralis*, 5. ed., 3 vols., Romae, 1908.

De Angelis, Philippus, *Praelectiones Iuris Canonici*, 5 vols. in 9, Romae—Parisiis, 1877-1891.

Decius, Philippus, *Super Decretalibus*, Lugduni, 1559.

Duballet, Blaise, *Cours Complet de Droit Canonique et de Jurisprudence Canonico-Civile*, 3 vols., Paris—Poitiers, 1898.

Fagnanus, Prosper, *Ius Canonicum seu Commentaria Absolutissima in Quinque Libros Decretalium*, 5 vols., Romae, 1661.

Fedele, Pio, *Discorso Generale sull'Ordinamento Canonico*, Padova: Casa Editrice Dottor Antonio Milan, 1941.

Ferraris, Lucius, *Prompta Bibliotheca, Canonica, Iuridica, Moralis, Theologica, necnon Ascetica, Polemica, Rubristica, Historica*, 9 vols., Romae, 1885-1899.

Geny, François, *Science et technique en droit privé positif*, 4 vols. in 8, Paris, 1914-1924.

Hammill, John Leo, *The Obligations of the Traveller According to Canon 14*, The Catholic University of America Canon Law Studies, n. 160, Washington, D.C.: The Catholic University of America Press, 1942.

Henrincx, Gulielmus, *Summa Theologiae Scholasticae et Moralis in Quatuor Partes Distributa*, 2. ed., 4 vols. in 3, Antverpiae, 1680.

Hollweck, Joseph, *Die kirchlichen Strafgesetze*, Mainz, 1899.

Hostiensis (Henricus de Segusio), *In Quinque Decretalium Gregorianarum Libros Commentaria*, Venetiis, 1581.

———, *Summa Aurea*, Venetiis, 1570.

Innocentius IV, *In Quinque Libros Decretalium Commentaria*, Venetiis, 1570.

Kilber, Henricus—Holtzclau, Thomas—Neubauer, Ignatius, *Theologia Dogmatica, Polemica, Scholastica, et Moralis in Alma Universitate Wirceburgensi*, 2. ed., 5 vols., Lutetiae Parisiorum, 1852-1854.

Lainé, Armand, *Introduction au Droit International Privé*, 2 vols., Paris, 1888.

Latini, Ioseph, *Iuris Criminalis Philosophici Summa Lineamenta*, Taurini—Romae: Marietti, 1924.

Laymann, Paulus, *Theologia Moralis*, 6. ed., 2 vols., Bambergae, 1669.

Lega, Michael, *Praelectiones in Textum Iuris Canonici de Iudiciis Ecclesiasticis*, 4 vols., Romae, 1896-1901.

Le Picard, René, *La Communauté de la Vie Conjugale*, Paris: Librairie du Receuil Sirey, 1930.

Lessius, Leonardus, *De Iustitia et Iure Ceterisque Virtutibus Cardinalibus Libri Quatuor*, Antverpiae, 1612.

Liguori, S. Alphonsus, *Theologia Moralis*, 14. ed., 4 vols., Bassani, 1836.

Lombardi, Carolus, *Iuris Canonici Privati Institutiones*, 2. ed., 2 vols., Romae, 1901.

Marc, P. Clemens, *Institutiones Morales Alphonsianae*, 2 vols., Romae, 1885.

Maroto, Philippus, *Institutiones Iuris Canonici ad normam novi Codicis*, 3. ed., 2 vols., Romae, 1919-1921.

Medina, Bartholomaeus de, *Expositio in I-IIae Angelici Doctoris D. Thomae Aquinatis*, Venetiis, 1590.

Medina, Ioannes de, *De Poenitentia, restitutione, et contractibus*, 2 vols. in 1, Ingolstadii, 1581.

Meehan, Andreas B., *Compendium Iuris Canonici*, Roffae, 1899.

Michiels, Gommarus, *De Delictis et Poenis*, Lublin: Universitas Catholica, 1934—

———, *Normae Generales Iuris Canonici*, 2. ed., 2 vols., Parisiis—Tornaci—Romae: Desclée et Socii, 1949.

Migne, Jacques Paul, *Patrologiae Cursus Completus, Series Latina*, 221 vols., Parisiis, 1844-1855.

Neumeyer, K., *Die gemeinrechtliche Entwickelung des internationalen Privat- und Strafrechts bis Bartolus*, 2 vols., München, 1901-1916.

Noldin, Hieronymus, *Summa Theologiae Moralis et Pastoralis*, 10. ed., 3 vols., Romae, 1912.

Onclin, Gulielmus, *De territoriali vel personali legis indole*, Gemblaci: J. Duculot, 1938.

Ojetti, Benedictus, *Synopsis Rerum Moralium et Iuris Pontificii*, 3. ed., 4 vols., Romae, 1909-1914.

Ottaviani, Alaphridus, *Compendium Iuris Publici Ecclesiastici*, 4. ed., Romae: Typis Polyglottis Vaticanis, 1954.

Pacelli, Eugène, *La Territorialité et Personalité des Lois particulièrement dans le Droit Canon*, Rome: Scientia Catholica, 1945.

Panormitanus (Nicholaus de Tudeschis), *Commentaria in Quinque Decretalium Libros*, 5 vols., Venetiis, 1588.

———, *Consilia Iuris, Quaestiones, et Praxis*, Venetiis, 1578.

Pillet, Antoine, *De l'Ordre Public en Droit International Privé*, Grenoble—Paris, 1890.

———, *Principes de Droit International Privé*, Paris, 1914.

——— —Niboyet, J.-P., *Manuel de Droit International Privé*, Paris, 1924.

Regatillo, Eduardus—Zalba, Marcellinus, *Theologiae Moralis Summa*, 3 vols., Matriti: Bibliotheca de Autores Cristianos, 1952-1954.

Reiffenstuel, Anacletus, *Theologia Moralis*, iam dudum edita, 2 vols., Bassani, 1773-1780.

*Repetitionum in Universas fere Iuris Canonici Partes Materiasque sane frequentiores Volumina Sex*, 6 vols., Venetiis, 1583.

Roberti, Franciscus, *De Delictis et Poenis*, 2. ed., Romae: apud Custodiam Librariam Pontificii Instituti Utriusque Iuris, 1944.

Rodrigo, Lucius, *Praelectiones Theologico-Morales Comillenses*, Series I, *Theologia Moralis Fundamentalis*, Tomus II, *Tractatus de Legibus*, Santander: Sal Terrae, 1944.

Sa, Emmanuel, *Aphorismi Confessariorum ex Variis Doctorum Sententiis*, ed. novissima, Lugduni, 1669.

Sanchez, Thomas, *Disputationum de Sancto Matrimonii Sacramento Libri Decem*, 3 vols., Venetiis, 1607.

Santi, Franciscus, *Praelectiones Iuris Canonici Iuxta Ordinem Decretalium Gregorii IX*, 5 vols. in 1, Ratisbonae—Neo-Eboraci—Cincinnati, 1886.

Savigny, Friedrich Carl Von, *System des heutigen Römischen Rechts*, 8 vols., Berlin, 1840-1849.

———, *Private International Law*, translated by William Guthrie, Edinburgh, 1869.

Schmalzgrueber, Franciscus, *Ius Canonicum Universum*, 6 vols. in 8, Romae, 1843.

Schmier, Franciscus, *Iurisprudentia Canonico-Civilis, seu Ius Canonicum Universum*, 2 vols., Venetiis, 1754.

Sirna, Iosephus, *De Notione Ordinis Publici in Ecclesia*, Pontificium Institutum Utriusque Iuris, Theses ad Lauream, n. 58, Romae: apud Custodiam Librariam Pontificii Instituti Utriusque Iuris, 1949.

Soto, Dominicus, *Commentarium in Quartum Sententiarum*, 2 vols., Venetiis, 1569.

Story, Joseph, *Commentaries on the Conflict of Laws*, 8. ed., Boston, 1883.

Suarez, Franciscus, *Opera Omnia*, 26 vols., Parisiis: Apud Ludovicum Vivés, 1856-1866. Vol. V, *De Legibus*, 1856; Vol. XIII, *De Virtute Religionis*, 1859; Vol. XXIII, *De Censuris*, 1861.

Tanquerey, Adolphus, *Synopsis Theologiae Moralis*, 3 vols., Tornaci—Neo-Eboraci, 1902-1905.

Valéry, J., *Manuel de Droit International Privé*, Paris, 1914.

Van Hove, Alphonsus, *Commentarium Lovaniense in Codicem Iuris Canonici*, 1 vol. in 5 toms., Mechliniae—Romae: H. Dessain, 1928-1939, Tom. I, *Prolegomena*, editio altera, 1945; Tom. II, *De Legibus Ecclesiasticis*, Mechliniae—Romae: H. Dessain, 1930.

Vermeersch, A.—Creusen, J., *Epitome Iuris Canonici*, 3 vols., Vol. I, 7. ed., 1949; Vol. II, 6. ed., 1940; Vol. III, 6. ed., 1946, Mechliniae—Romae: H. Dessain.

Weiss, André, *Traité Théorique et Practique de Droit International Privé*, 4 vols., Paris, 1892-1901.

Wenger, Leopold, *Institutes of the Roman Law of Civil Procedure*, rev. ed., translated by Otis Harrison Fisk, New York: Veritas, 1940.

Wernz, Franciscus X., *Ius Decretalium*, 6 vols., Romae—Prati, 1898-1914.

——— —Vidal, P., *Ius Canonicum ad Codicis Normam Exactum*, 7 vols., in 8, Romae: apud Aedes Universitatis Gregorianae, 1923-1938; Vol. I, 2. ed., 1951; Vol. VII, 2. ed., 1951.

Wolff, Martin, *Private International Law*, London: Oxford University Press, 1945.

ARTICLES

Bodenheimer, Edgar, "The Public Policy Exception in Private International Law: A Reappraisal in the Light of Legal Philosophy," *Seminar,* XII (1954), 51-66.

Fallon, M. J., "The Obligation of Wearing Clerical Dress During Holidays," *Irish Ecclesiastical Record,* XLIX (1937), 499-501.

Kinane, J., "'Peregrini' and the laws which take care of public order," *Irish Ecclesiastical Record,* XLIII (1934), 113-125.

Le Picard, René, "La Notion d'Ordre Public en Droit Canonique," *Nouvelle Revue Théologique,* LV (1928), 352-372.

———, "Bien public," *Dictionnaire de Droit Canonique,* II (1937), col. 826-835.

Mancini, Pasquale Stanislao, "De l'utilité de rendre obligatoire pour tous les États, sous la forme d'un ou de plusieurs traités internationaux, un certain nombres de règles générales du Droit international privé pour assurer la décision uniforme des conflits entre les différentes législations civilles et criminelles," *Journal du Droit International Privé,* I (1874), 221-239; 285-304.

Roelker, Edward, "The Traveller and the Local Statute," *The Jurist,* II (1942), 105-119.

Van Hove, Alphonsus, "Leges Quae Ordini Publico Consulunt," *Ephemerides Theologicae Lovanienses,* I (1924), 153-167.

PERIODICALS

*Dictionnaire de Droit Canonique,* Paris: Letouzey et Ané, 1924—

*Ephemerides Theologicae Lovanienses,* Lovanii, 1924—

*Irish Ecclesiastical Record,* Dublin: Browne and Nolan, 1864—

*Journal du Droit International Privé,* Paris, 1874—

*Jurist, The,* Washington, D.C., 1941—

*Nouvelle Revue Théologique,* Paris, 1869—

*Seminar,* Washington, D.C., 1943-1956.


## ABBREVIATIONS

| | |
|---|---|
| *AAS* | —*Acta Apostolicae Sedis* |
| Auth. | —*Authenticum* |
| C | —*Codex Iustiniani* |
| D | —*Digesta; Decreta Authentica Congregationis Sacrorum Rituum* |
| *DDC* | —*Dictionnaire de Droit Canonique* |
| *ETL* | —*Ephemerides Theologicae Lovanienses* |
| *IER* | —*Irish Ecclesiastical Record* |
| *JDIP* | —*Journal du Droit International Privé* |
| *MPL* | —Migne, *Patrologiae Cursus Completus, Series Latina* |
| Nov. | —*Novellae* |
| *NRT* | —*Nouvelle Revue Théologique* |
| S.R.C. | —*Sacrorum Rituum Congregatio* |

# INDEX

## BIOGRAPHICAL NOTE

John Henry Hackett was born in Fall River, Massachusetts, on May 12, 1926. He attended the Sacred Heart School in that city and Monsignor James Coyle High School in Taunton. From 1943 to 1945 he studied at Saint Charles College, Catonsville, Maryland, and in March, 1945, he entered Saint John's Seminary in Brighton, Massachusetts. In 1950 he received the degree of Bachelor of Arts from Saint John's Seminary and, on June 3, 1950, was ordained to the Priesthood at the Cathedral of Saint Mary of the Assumption, Fall River.

His first assignment after ordination was to Saint Thomas More Church in Somerset, Massachusetts. He served there as an assistant until coming to the School of Canon Law of the Catholic University of America in September, 1955. He received the degree of Bachelor of Canon Law in 1956, and the Licentiate in Canon Law in 1957.

## CANON LAW STUDIES*

392. Adams, Rev. Donald E., A.B., J.C.L., The truth required in the *preces* for rescripts.
393. Bégin, Rev. Raymond F., A.B., S.T.L., J.C.L., Natural law and positive law.
394. Clancy, Rev. Walter B., A.B., J.C.L., The rights and ceremonies of sacred ordination.
395. Cox, Rev. Ronald J., S.T.L., J.C.L., A study of the juridic status of laymen in the writing of the medieval canonists.
396. Demers, Rev. Francis L., O.M.I., A.B., J.C.L., Temporal administration of the religious house in a non-exempt clerical pontifical institute.
397. Dziadosz, Rev. Henry J., M.A., S.T.L., J.C.L., The provisions of the Decree "Spiritus Sancti munera": the law for the extraordinary minister of confirmation.
398. Gerhardt, Rev. Bernard C., A.B., S.T.L., J.C.L., Interpretation of rescripts.
399. Hackett, Rev. John H., A.B., J.C.L., The concept of public order.
400. Murphy, Rev. Richard J., O.M.I., S.T.L., J.C.L., The canonico-juridical status of a communist.
401. O'Connor, Rev. David, M.S.SS.T., J.C.L., Parochial relations and co-operation of the religious and secular clergy.

*For a complete list of the available numbers of this series apply to the Catholic University of America Press, 620 Michigan Avenue, N.E., Washington (17), D.C., for a general catalogue.

www.ingramcontent.com/pod-product-compliance
Lightning Source LLC
LaVergne TN
LVHW050200080826
844660LV00012B/323
* 9 7 8 0 8 1 3 2 2 5 5 9 3 *